GUIDE TO

SMART WEDDING PLANNING

Edna Dratch-Parker & Jeri Solomon

Cover design and inside hand lettering: Jyotirmayee Patra
Illustrations: Shana Cinquegrana
Layout design: Lauren Phipps

Publisher's Cataloging-in-Publication Data
(Prepared by Cassidy Cataloguing Services, Inc.)

Names:	Dratch-Parker, Edna, author. | Solomon, Jeri, author.
Title:	Guide to smart wedding planning / Edna Dratch-Parker & Jeri Solomon.
Description:	First edition. | Stoneham, MA: Real Deal Wedding Insiders, [2022]
Identifiers:	ISBN: 979-8-9865888-0-3 (softcover) ISBN: 979-8-9865888-1-0 (ebook)
Subjects:	LCSH: Weddings--Planning--Handbooks, manuals, etc. | Wedding etiquette--Handbooks, manuals, etc. | Brides--Handbooks, manuals, etc. | Bridegrooms. | Betrothal. | Marriage customs and rites. | Weddings--Costs. | Finance, Personal. | Wedding attendants. | Weddings--Equipment and supplies. | Wedding supplies and services industry.
Classification:	LCC: HQ745.D73 2022 | DDC: 395.2/2--dc23

In memory of Jeri's aunt,

Eleanor Henkoff,

and in honor of Edna's aunt,

Mary Dratch Rosenfield,

the matriarchs who adored a

great family celebration.

Contents

Introduction   i

CHAPTER 1: ENGAGEMENT: THE PERFECT STORM

  2 SMART Wedding Planning

  5 The Five REAL DEAL Truths of Planning a Wedding

 10 Summary

CHAPTER 2: IDENTIFYING YOUR WEDDING COMMITTEE

 16 Building Your Wedding Committee

 20 Establishing the Rules of Engagement with Your Bankroller

 23 Handle Your VIPs with Care

 23 The Confidant: Your Secret Weapon

 25 A Word About Judgers

 26 The REAL DEAL about Wedding Committees

 29 Summary

CHAPTER 3: CREATING YOUR WEDDING VISION

 32 How Weddings Have Changed

 36 Three Steps to Creating Your Wedding Vision

 53 Summary

CHAPTER 4: BUILDING YOUR REAL DEAL WEDDING BUDGET

 56 Time to Talk Money

 58 Creating a Realistic Budget and Sticking to It

 60 Building Your REAL DEAL Wedding Budget

 76 Summary

CHAPTER 5: **BUILDING YOUR GUEST LIST
AND CHOOSING YOUR VENUE**

80   The Guest List

84   The Wedding Venue

87   Venue Categories and Questions to Ask

92   Summary

CHAPTER 6: **ASSEMBLING YOUR VENDOR TEAM**

96   What a Wedding Planner Can Do for You

100   Your Vendor Team

103   Vetting Your Vendors

108   Getting the Most Out of Your Vendors

109   Weighing the Trade-Offs: Seasoned Professional
vs. Newbie Professional vs. DIY

113   Sealing the Deal

114   Unexpected Costs

116   Summary

CHAPTER 7: **THE BIG DAY**

121   Day-Of Management and Logistics

124   The Who: Your Point People

127   Tips for Staying Present

130   Summary

Congratulations! You're engaged! You're embarking on the immense project of planning a wedding. Are you thinking you don't know where to start? Feeling pressure that you have that one chance to make this important day perfect? That's normal. You can't expect to be an expert at wedding planning. The good news is we are the experts and we're here to help.

This book is different. We know everyone is writing, talking, posting, blogging, and pinning about weddings, but we have a unique perspective. We've seen hundreds of weddings and have the inside scoop because we work, live, and breathe the wedding business.

There's something special about being part of a momentous family celebration—no matter how big or small. Every client we work with entrusts us with their special day and we take that very seriously. We're a part of creating an event that brings families and friends together to celebrate important milestones. That's a big deal! It's the ultimate celebration, and we think it's important to help our clients have the best experience possible. We're both driven by a passion for helping people bring their wedding visions into reality.

Edna, founder and creative director of EFD Creative—Event Planning & Design, brings her unique blend of experience as an artist, entrepreneur, and creative director to each and every wedding she's produced for the more than a decade. A graduate of Maine College of Art & Design, her approach to events comes from her desire to create a cohesive and visually engaging experience. She aligns her artistic sensibility with her professionalism to create a wedding experience that is memorable, distinctive, and seamless. Edna has received a number of industry honors, including "Wedding of the Year" from the National Association of Catering and Events (NACE), "Social Event Planner of the Year" from BizBash, and "Trendsetter of the Year" from *Wedding Planner* magazine. Her weddings have been featured in national and regional publications.

Jeri, owner of Jeri Solomon Floral Design is a graduate of University of Pennsylvania. She parlayed her entrepreneurial spirit with her early love of flowers into a business that has allowed her to be creative and thrive in the Boston market for over 25 years. Jeri's motto is "Weddings are stressful; flowers shouldn't be." She believes in providing each of her customers not just gorgeous floral arrangements, but also exceptional service, attention to detail, and impeccable design. Her work has been featured in numerous publications including *Boston Weddings*, *Flower* magazine, *The Knot* magazine, *Modern Luxury Weddings: Boston*, and *Grace Ormonde Wedding Style*. As one of the founding members of the prestigious Boston Wedding Group, Jeri has served in various leadership roles including president.

Together we have wisdom and want to share it with you. This book isn't about hairstyle selections, dress options, or which flowers are available in the season you're getting married. It's about the difficult, uncomfortable parts like money, family dynamics, and the amount of work and planning it really takes to create your wedding. We give you the true insight needed to pull off your awesome, once-in-a-lifetime wedding while keeping your sanity. We've built reputations based on honesty and straight talk. We're going to do the same in this book. It's not just the pretty stuff—it's the REAL DEAL!

OUR FRIENDSHIP

We've been collaborating on weddings for many years, and through our shared experiences, our professional partnership extended into a strong personal friendship. It's this bond, along with our zeal for weddings, that inspired the book you're reading.

We often joke that we're "sisters from another mister," and it's not far from the truth: We grew up in neighboring Massachusetts towns and we have two sisters each. Both of our fathers served as military doctors while stationed in France. We were raised with similar beliefs and values. Our husbands are both named Jim, and our aunts, Eleanor and Mary, met one another and became friends at the same retirement community! The list goes on.

This book was written by real wedding professionals who work in the trenches and can give you real-life advice that is practical, proven, and actionable. Think of us as your wedding planning gurus. You can trust us to share our wisdom with both compassion and a healthy dose of real talk.

With that in mind, come take this ride with us—we'll steer you in the right direction and get you through this whirlwind journey of wedding planning.

We are the REAL DEAL WEDDING INSIDERS!

* * *

We celebrate all couples regardless of their gender, race, ethnicity, sexual orientation or identity who want to formalize their relationship with marriage. This book is intended for everyone planning a wedding.

CHAPTER

1

Engagement

THE PERFECT STORM

Planning a wedding can be extremely stressful. There's no other period in your life where the expenditure of time, money, and emotions churn together to create a perfect storm as much as when you're trying to create The Most Important Day of Your Life!

Being engaged is one of the most exciting times in your life, but it can cause some unexpected challenges, and at times it can get downright chaotic. So, let's help you get organized and get into a more manageable mindset.

Your life is already busy, and now you've got to find time to plan a wedding, with all the emotions and multitude of details that come with it. We know you want to make wise choices from the get-go. And that's what we're here to help with.

SMART Wedding Planning

A lot needs to happen in order for you to realize your ideal wedding, no matter how big or small it may be. To get there, you've got to be *SMART* about your decisions. Your choices should be:

S **Specific** to your priorities and needs

M **Manageable** within your budget, time frame, and comfort zone

A **Articulated** clearly communicated to family and vendors

R **Realistic** of expectations

T **Timely** made with enough information and with enough time to execute them

This book gives you the *SMART* approach to develop and refine your wedding vision, bring it to life within your particular budget and timeline, and manage your family and vendors to get the best results.

SMART wedding planning includes the Three Cs of what it *really* takes to produce the wedding you want: Communication, Comprehension, and Calculation. You will need to:

- **Communicate** with your family and partner, as well as your vendors.
- **Comprehend** what it takes to produce the wedding you envision.
- **Calculate** the real cost of your wedding.

Almost from the moment you announce, "We're engaged!" the tension starts to mount. Within days (or hours), the questions start coming: When's the date? What's your color scheme? Do you have a venue/photographer/dress?

Your stress level rises as to-do lists start swirling in your head. Your first instinct might be to try to get a head start by making appointments to try on dresses or visit venues. Our advice? The first thing you should do is press pause.

Wedding planning requires you to look at the big picture. Every decision you make, from the venue you choose to the size of your guest list to the number of bridesmaids, will affect other decisions down the road. This road may be new to you, and it's difficult to know what lies ahead, so it's important to take your time and plan your journey.

If you're going to have the wedding you envision, then shopping for your dress or finding your venue is not step one. These are all exciting and important aspects of planning but prioritizing, budgeting, and research need to be done before those steps are started.

Once you're engaged, hit the pause button, take a deep breath and look at the big picture. Get real with yourself and ask the following questions: What's truly important to you? What are your priorities? What are your financial circumstances? Then, ask the same questions of your spouse-to-be, your parents, and anyone else involved in the wedding planning. This should all happen before you take any other action.

SMART wedding planning means setting expectations and navigating the journey (and potholes) with the family, friends, and vendors who'll be helping to bring your vision to life. One of the biggest mistakes we see is couples who don't think about the repercussions of their choices until they're too far down the wedding planning road—when it's almost impossible to change course. The results? Feelings get hurt, too much money is spent on the wrong things, and stress levels get out of control.

You might be thinking, *But Edna and Jeri, I already know what type of wedding I want and where it will take place.* That's good. Hold on to those thoughts. But don't do anything about them yet.

There are three things you need to do in the early stages of planning, in this (very important) order:

1. **Identify your Wedding Committee:** Your Wedding Committee is the group of people who have influence on your decisions (whether you like it or not).
2. **Establish your vision:** The vision is the overall look, feel, and experience you want to create for your wedding.
3. **Set your REAL DEAL budget:** This budget is what it will actually cost to execute your vision.

We'll go into each of these tasks in the following chapters, but for now, know this: if you can tackle these three things, the rest of the planning process—including dealing with difficult people, choosing the right venue and vendors, and making choices on décor—will become a whole lot easier and more enjoyable.

Before we jump into more details of wedding planning, though, let's take a look at a few common reasons why this process can make anyone a little anxious.

The Five REAL DEAL Truths
Of Planning A Wedding

1. WEDDINGS BRING OUT THE "ZILLA" IN EVERYONE

Brides get a bad rap. Maybe it's Hollywood or reality TV shows, but the tired cliché of the demanding "Bridezilla" is widespread in our culture. Sure, some brides can be incredibly difficult, but the "Bridezilla" mentality is not limited to the bride. "Zillas" are gender-neutral and come in all shapes and sizes. *No one* is immune.

You'll quickly learn (maybe you already have) that everyone has opinions and ideas about what's best for you. You'll want to stay focused on what is right for you and your partner.

Planning is not going to be a smooth process. For instance, you may think you're arguing about flowers but at the root of the fight are some unresolved issues that have been plaguing your family for years. Weddings bring out both the best and worst in people because weddings are emotional–*really emotional*–and many long-dormant issues can suddenly resurface.

Maybe you're thinking, *But I'm not like that. I would never get that emotional.* Some couples manage to keep the drama at a minimum. But it's always easier to watch–and judge–from afar. When it's *your* wedding at stake, it's a whole different ball game. Often people you thought you knew intimately start acting like strangers, behaving in ways you never saw coming. Nothing about wedding planning is as simple or straightforward as you believed it would be.

Luckily, if you keep a cool head and try to see others' perspectives, you can avoid the pitfalls of the overzealous Zilla–even your own inner Zilla!

2. IT WILL TEST YOUR MARRIAGE AND RELATIONSHIPS

Wedding planning is a true test of your future marriage. You're packing a lifetime of experiences into an engagement period that lasts an average of 16 months.[1] So many skeletons come out of the closet, you'll think it's Halloween—hidden agendas, financial worries, sibling rivalries, jealous friends, ancient family dramas, and more.

You're confronted with combining families that have possibly never met as well as dealing with others' constraints and expectations—issues you may have never noticed before. Differences between you and your future spouse's family, whether they're cultural, socioeconomic, religious, or political, can affect many wedding planning decisions. If you fail to take these sensitivities into account, people will be unhappy. When you merge two lives and families, conflicts can come up. Wedding planning packs it all into a compressed timeframe—the good, the bad, and the . . . well . . . ugly.

You may discover what you want in a wedding is very different from what your family or partner wants. You may dream of an intimate wedding with your closest family and friends, but your partner has a large extended family who wants to party till dawn at a blowout event. Perhaps you're more reserved and don't relish the spotlight, while your spouse-to-be is devising a grand plan for a funny dance routine with his fraternity brothers. These are not insignificant issues. Everything about you and your future spouse—your personalities, values, family dynamics—comes into play during the wedding planning process and it matters.

While there may not be a way to avoid conflicts entirely, you can limit the fallout by staying in constant communication with your partner, your family, your friends, and your vendors. Remember to not only voice your needs and wants, but to take others' into account as well. A little compromise can go a long way in these circumstances.

....

[1] Maddy Sims, "Here's the Average Length of Engagement for Couples," accessed March 2, 2022 https://www.theknot.com/content/average-engagement-length

3. MORE OPTIONS = MORE STRESS

A generation ago, getting married wasn't as complicated. In previous generations, couples got the venue, ordered some flowers, decided on chicken or beef as the entrée, and hired a band or DJ.

In the last 25 years, the wedding industry has undergone a major renaissance due to the internet and social media. It's never been easier to peer into the lives of others. Their vacations, parties, and weddings are broadcast, pinned, tagged, shared, and followed through every possible channel. Reality TV has given us an inside view into celebrity lifestyles, which for better or worse, has influenced everything in our culture, including weddings. While most of us can't afford a celebrity-style wedding, that doesn't stop the images we see from leading to higher expectations for our own weddings. The wedding industry has evolved to satisfy our increasingly high demands.

From signature cocktails to wedding websites, hashtags, custom logos, and multimedia entertainment, weddings are more personalized and complex than ever. The sheer number of choices involved is enough to make even the most ambitious and organized couple feel overwhelmed. The good news is that at weddings, your guests get a unique experience that reflects you and your partner's personalities. The bad news is that all this uniqueness comes at a price—more decisions mean more stress.

4. IT'S A LOT MORE WORK THAN YOU THINK IT WILL BE

You may have organized dozens of successful birthday and anniversary parties, and your multitasking skills duly impress your friends. But planning a wedding is on a whole different level.

For one, it's more emotional. A wedding is one of the most important milestones in your life. You want it to be perfect. At the same time, you're dealing with other people's expectations and desires. This requires tough compromises and decisions along the way.

Also, weddings are no longer a one-day, once-and-done event. They

Planning a wedding requires managing a budget, hiring vendors, and making countless decisions. It can be as time consuming as a second job.

can last several days, with different celebrations occurring that encompass more than just the wedding ceremony and reception. It's also an opportunity for a couple to show who they are to their family and friends, as well as whoever might be watching via social media.

Lastly, the stakes for a wedding are much higher than any other event. This is THE day, the one you'll document, photograph, and share with your children and grandchildren. There's no do-over here. It's not like burning the turkey at Thanksgiving, when you have the chance to make another one next year. It's one day you'll relive for years to come. You want to make certain it's a memorable one—for the right reasons. No one wants to be the couple who falls into the pool, memorialized on YouTube forever.

The average couple will work with 10 vendors and spend 12 hours a week planning their wedding[2], and that's not including any unique touches. And while your friends may rave about this photographer or that band, we still recommend researching an average of three vendors in each category before hiring one (more on that process in chapters 5 and 6). All this is in addition to time spent browsing online and getting recommendations before narrowing down your choices.

5. IT'S GOING TO COST MORE THAN YOU THINK

This one is a toughie. Nothing makes people more uncomfortable than talking about money. Everyone knows weddings are expensive, but couples seem to have blinders on when it comes to planning their own.

When you become engaged, you get introduced to an industry you may have been completely unfamiliar with previously. Couples get sticker shock when they find out how much flowers, invitations, specialized lighting, transportation, and entertainment cost. It's incredibly easy to blow your budget if you don't factor everything in from the start.

So how do you know what you want or need in the first place? That's what we're here for! Keep reading.

The average cost of a wedding in the United States is around $30,000, and nearly 60% of couples end up spending more than they originally planned.[3]

[2] SWNS, "Engaged couples spend an enormous amount of time planning their weddings, study finds," February 21, 2019, https://www.foxnews.com/lifestyle/engaged-couples-spend-an-enormous-amount-of-time-planning-their-weddings-study-finds.

[3] "2020 Wedding Report," accessed July, 22, 2020, https://go.weddingwire.com/newlywed-report.

Summary

When it comes to your wedding, you want to make *SMART* choices:

S Specific to your priorities and needs

M Manageable within your budget, time frame, and comfort zone

A Articulated clearly communicated to family and vendors

R Realistic of expectations

T Timely made with enough information and with enough time to execute them

Much of the stress of wedding planning can be avoided by focusing on the Three C's of SMART wedding planning: Communication, Comprehension, and Calculation.

The first thing to do after getting engaged is to pause before making any decisions and follow these three steps:

1. **Identify your Wedding Committee:** the people involved in the decisions and planning.
2. **Establish your vision:** the overall experience you want to create.
3. **Set your REAL DEAL budget:** what it actually costs to produce your vision.

Beware the Five REAL DEAL Truths of Planning a Wedding:

1. Weddings Bring Out the "Zilla" in Everyone
2. It Will Test Your Marriage and Relationships
3. More Options = More Stress
4. It's a Lot More Work Than You Think It Will Be
5. It's Going To Cost More Than You Think

CHAPTER
2

IDENTIFYING YOUR
WEDDING

Committee

The biggest misstatement about weddings is: *It's your day; you get to do whatever you want.* The truth is, your wedding day belongs not only to you but also your family.

In the non-stop world we live in, it's easy to forget how intensely momentous and far-reaching an occasion a wedding truly is. Everyone in your family is affected. The majority of couples gather family and friends, hold a ceremony, and have some type of a celebration. The details will vary across religions, regions, or social groups, but the core elements remain the same.

The reality is that wedding planning doesn't happen in a bubble. It happens by committee, and your opinion can sometimes be the last one that matters. People say, "It's your wedding. Do what you want." We agree in theory, but we also know you get what you pay for, which leads us to ask, Who is paying for your wedding? We also know the squeaky wheel gets the grease. So we ask, Who will be the loudest/strongest in expressing their opinions? Wedding planning, like marriage, is a series of compromises.

You probably have specific ideas about your wedding, but we guarantee as soon as you utter, "I'd like to . . ." you'll be bombarded with opinions by everyone within earshot. This isn't necessarily a bad thing. Most people have your best interests at heart. What they suggest just might not be what *you* want.

We've seen couples become very upset when they realize their happy little bubble of "us" gets ripped open by other people's needs in the process of wedding planning. You might have to accommodate a longstanding family tradition, a beloved aunt, or a parent who's holding the purse strings. Navigating the waters of "what everyone else wants" is tricky and can be emotionally draining. That's why, if you're serious about keeping your sanity during this process, it's imperative to take control from the start.

The first step of taking control is accepting the need for a Wedding Committee and identifying who the players are going to be. Don't even think about dress shopping, looking at venues, or selecting your wedding date before completing this step. Some of you will do these things anyway, but we *highly* recommend you don't commit to anything before identifying your committee.

We suggest you sit down with your partner and take stock of the important people in your life. Make a list. The exercise may seem silly, but trust us, the effort you put in now will save you time, money, and grief down the road. Though you may have (finally) figured out your own family, you may not be fully aware yet of all the dynamics in your spouse-to-be's family. Most people are surprised by what they find. This exercise sets up a framework so you and your partner can agree on how much importance you want to give certain individuals during the planning process. Your goal is to become united as a couple before bringing family into the mix.

You know the saying, "United we stand, divided we fall"? Truer words were never spoken about wedding planning. It is essential that you are on the same page as your partner.

Weddings are notorious for exposing resentments and vulnerable feelings. Uncover potential issues early so you can strategize together how to minimize their impact.

Building Your Wedding Committee

The first thing to understand is your Wedding Committee is not your wedding *party*. While there may be overlap between the two, these are entirely different groups. Here's how we break it down:

WEDDING PARTY: Party = Fun! These are the people you want by your side on your big day. They are your closest family and friends who have special roles, including best man, maid of honor, mother of the bride, flower girl, etc. They are the ones who will wear special clothes and walk down the aisle for the ceremony. Many will be involved in helping plan your wedding and throwing parties in your honor (e.g., engagement party, bridal shower, bachelor and bachelorette parties).

WEDDING COMMITTEE: Committee = Work. These are the key power players. These people have varying degrees of financial and emotional influence on you and your future spouse. Their opinions matter and they are on the committee whether you like it or not.

Remember when you first got engaged? There was a brief period of bliss and then the questions started. They came from everyone—family, friends, your boss, even your barista. When are you thinking of getting married? What type of wedding do you want? Have you thought about bridesmaids? From the start, people try to influence your decisions. It happens quite naturally and usually with good intentions. It's important to figure out whose opinions matter enough to have a seat at the decision-making table and whose don't.

This is why identifying your committee comes first. Thoughtful and measured steps at this stage can help you expertly manage people's expectations without causing a family feud. We're not saying you have to hide or minimize your engagement. By all means, shout it from the rooftops! Blast it across the social media stratosphere! What we're saying is don't make any plans or commit to any decisions until you've completed this first step.

Over the years, we've identified three main types of influencers who will be on your committee:

THE BANKROLLER(S): This person or persons holds the purse strings to your wedding dreams. This is where wedding fantasy meets practical reality. You can't have a wedding without someone financing it. You may be footing some (or all) of the bill yourself, but fully self-financed weddings are still the minority (only 14% of couples pay for their weddings entirely on their own.)[4] For the majority of couples, other people control the finances. How will you deal with those people? How involved will they be? Are they a silent backer or a micromanager? Do you have to meet certain conditions? Knowing how to approach and effectively communicate with your Bankrollers is critical.

THE VIP(S): Their needs are at the top of your list. These are the people whose opinions or circumstances matter, even though they aren't necessarily contributing financially. They could be a nonpaying parent, sibling, best friend, grandparent, or other family member. Because of this person, you might do things differently than you originally thought. For example, you might consent to a religious ceremony to honor your grandmother or rethink that beach venue because the terrain is too difficult for your cousin's motorized wheelchair. You care about them and consider their needs and requests.

THE CONFIDANT(S): These people are the easiest to identify. They love and support you unconditionally, and you can share your excitement as well as vent your frustrations with them. In return, they'll give you practical advice and have your back. The Confidant might be your partner, best man, or maid of honor, but not necessarily. It's the person you trust most with your secrets, the one who has your back and serves as your sounding board.

[4]Businesswire. "On Average, Couples Work Toward Four Additional Financial Goals While Saving for Their Wedding." May 13, 2021. https://www.businesswire.com/news/home/20210513005592/en/On-Average-Couples-Work-Toward-Four-Additional-Financial-Goals-While-Saving-for-Their-Wedding

Within each of these categories, you'll find Judgers—the most notorious of your guests. These folks can be bossy and passive-aggressive. They have the power to turn a joyous experience into a miserable one. It could be a bridesmaid who got married last year and "knows everything," or a family member who's miffed about her role in the wedding. You might have a long and complicated history with the Judgers, so tread carefully. The last thing you need is unwanted drama. Hopefully you're one of the lucky ones who doesn't have a Judger in your crew. However, it's best to be honest with yourself and your partner about who these people are (or might be) so you can put a game plan in place for how to deal with them.

It is possible people will fall into multiple categories. You may have a future mother-in-law who is both a VIP and a Judger or a cousin who is a Confidant and a VIP. Once you sit down with your partner and create your lists, you'll start to identify potential concerns. **Note:** This list is fluid. Someone might not reveal themselves as a Judger until you get further down the road.

This process of creating your Wedding Committee forces you to think proactively about how to get the support you need while minimizing any friction. It empowers you to make decisions while being realistic. If your mother is financing your wedding, then she gets to have input. If you don't want her input, then you may think about not accepting her money. Alternatively, if your mother is a VIP and a Judger but not a Bankroller, you should take her feelings into consideration, but the final decision is yours.

IDENTIFYING YOUR WEDDING COMMITTEE

NAME	COMMITTEE ROLE			JUDGER?	NOTES
Your Family	Bankroller	VIP	Confidant		
(Sample) Your Mother	✓	✓		YES	My mother and I aren't particularly close, but she's chipping in for the wedding and her opinions matter to me.
Spouse's Father		✓		NO	Sam's father lost his job and can't afford to help with the wedding, and he has certain health needs that should be taken into consideration.

NAME	COMMITTEE ROLE			JUDGER?	NOTES
Your Family	Bankroller	VIP	Confidant		

NAME	COMMITTEE ROLE			JUDGER?	NOTES
Spouse's Family	Bankroller	VIP	Confidant		

Establishing The Rules Of Engagement With Your Bankroller

YOUR PARTNER IN PLANNING

Once you've created your list, the next step is to initiate honest conversations with your Bankrollers. They're providing the monetary support, so it's important to establish "Rules of Engagement." Take the time to connect with them and start setting expectations. Show gratitude. These people are giving you money for a wedding. It's a gift, and you should treat it as such. This helps open the lines of communication.

We suggest, if possible, meeting with your Bankrollers in person when talking about money, especially large amounts. It's important to see the nuances in the conversation, especially facial expressions and body language. Of course, sometimes meeting in person is not possible, as people may live far apart. If this is your situation, then talk via video call so you can see each other. Give this conversation the importance it's due. You're setting the tone for how you'll work together going forward. Your Bankrollers will appreciate it, even if they don't say it.

Often, the initial meeting will include a combination of Bankroller and VIP (for example, one parent is paying, while the other is helping to plan). If you have multiple Bankrollers, you'll need to schedule a meeting with each one.

Even if you and your partner are self-financing your wedding, don't skip this step. How you discuss finances with your partner is often an indicator of how you'll operate in marriage. There's no time like the present to establish your own Rules of Engagement. It's healthy and creates a positive financial relationship.

Discussing the budget is by far one of the most delicate issues in wedding planning. Often the Bankroller has a number in mind, but you don't know how much your vision will cost yet. You'll start to feel each other out. The Bankroller may offer a set amount, or they might be flexible depending on priorities. There might be expectations and conditions attached to the money that aren't always obvious. Be sure to find out what those expectations and conditions are before proceeding with the planning process.

During your meeting with the Bankroller(s), it's important to remember the biggest factors that influence your budget: guest count (that is, how many people you're inviting), venue (the location will determine about half of the cost of the wedding, as well as the overall look and feel of the entire event), and priorities (what's most important to you, your partner, and your Bankrollers). We will go into more detail on these topics in chapters 4 and 5.

GIVE YOUR BANKROLLER AN EXAMPLE OF WHAT YOU'RE THINKING

"I'd love a casual, intimate wedding in the countryside, perhaps 70 to 80 people."

"I've always dreamed of getting married at the beach and having everyone stay for a long weekend to celebrate."

"I want a huge reception in the city with a great band and lots of dancing. I'm thinking around 150 to 200 people."

The Bankroller's feedback will let you know of any potential issues immediately. Perhaps the number of guests you're thinking of is unrealistic or your Bankroller wants a more centrally located wedding. The time to hash out these differences is before you start planning.

This may sound like a no-brainer, but believe us when we say it's extremely common for couples to waste time and energy looking at venues and talking with vendors without anyone else's input. They make assumptions based on what they want and are blindsided when they discover their Bankroller wants something else. This inevitably leads to conflict and financial strain. Be smart—save yourself regret and meet with your Bankroller and communicate *before* you do anything else. That's why we call it *SMART* wedding planning.

Laila

When Laila got engaged, she was thrilled to start planning her beach wedding. She loved the idea of saying her vows with her feet in the sand and taking photos by the water. She already had a few locations in mind when she met with her parents (the Bankrollers) to discuss the budget. Her parents always assumed Laila would get married at the local hotel where they celebrated many family gatherings. They were friends with the manager, it would be easy to arrange, and all their friends and family lived locally. Laila envisioned a more casual wedding and expected her parents would let her get married at a place of her choice. She hadn't taken into consideration their priorities, which were having the convenience of working with people they knew and the traditional atmosphere of the hotel ballroom.

Laila and her parents were at an impasse. But since mom and dad were the Bankrollers, Laila wanted to respect their wishes. She took the time to understand their concerns and addressed each one while making a convincing case for wanting a venue that would be unique to her family. Upon further reflection, she realized the reason she wanted a beach wedding was that she preferred water views and thought a beach was the only way to obtain a casual, breezy vibe. She made some adjustments to her vision. She looked for and found a function hall by a lake with water views and a conventional reception area closer to home that would appeal to her parents. When her parents met the staff, they were impressed with the professionalism. She made her parents feel comfortable every step of the way, financially and psychologically. She established monthly meetings, kept them in the loop, and let her mother choose when and how she wanted to get involved. It was a good compromise, and in the end, Laila got her ideal wedding, with her parents' full support complete with photos of the wedding party on the sandy beach by the lake.

It doesn't matter if your wedding costs $5,000 or $500,000, the dynamics are the same. Someone else may be paying for your wedding, and they have their own opinions and preferences. You need to determine what they are and how to work with them.

DISCUSS HOW INVOLVED YOUR BANKROLLER WANTS TO BE

Some Bankrollers will be more hands-off, but some Bankrollers want to be included in everything from the cake tasting to the table linen selection. Find out what your Bankroller prefers. Understand their point of view. By giving your Bankroller this opportunity upfront, you'll be able to shape your vision with their support and create a more positive experience for everyone.

Handle Your VIPs With Care

VIPs may not be paying for your wedding, but they can have as much or more influence than your Bankrollers. Maybe one parent is footing the bill, and the other has the final say, which makes them both VIP and de facto Bankroller.

You know the power players in your family, but what about in your future spouse's family? Have a talk with your partner to determine who their VIPs are and why.

Some VIPs require extra TLC. If their approval is important, then have the same discussion with them you had with your Bankrollers. They might have a different perspective or highlight issues you hadn't considered. Though ultimately it's you and your spouse, as well as your Bankrollers, that have the final say in the big decisions, getting feedback from your VIPs early on is vital to ensure a smooth planning process.

The Confidant: Your Secret Weapon

Your Confidant is a special and valued ally in your journey. They can:
- Give honest feedback and be a voice of reason
- Provide emotional support
- Take on tasks you'd rather not do yourself
- Listen without judgment

Relying on your Confidant doesn't mean they're at your beck and call. Their lives are busy too!

In short, Confidants are a godsend. They love you and often go the extra mile beyond their official role in your wedding (if they have one). Bring them into the planning process early and make certain they know how much you appreciate them. Share your concerns about the Judgers, VIPs, and Bankrollers. However, remember to be cognizant of their time and needs as well. While they are willing to be there for you when you need them, it's important not to take advantage of their generosity!

REAL DEAL LIFE EXAMPLE #2:

Michelle, Lillian and Sasha

Michelle loved her mother, Lillian, (who was the Bankroller), but they had a difficult relationship and frequently butted heads. Michelle wanted to get married in an industrial loft with a hip downtown feel. Lillian wanted Michelle to get married at her local temple where her siblings got married. Michelle knew herself well enough to know that given her history with her mother, she was not the best person to sell Lillian on the loft idea. She enlisted the help of her sister Sasha, her Confidant. Sasha had an easier relationship with their mother and tended to stay calm when things heated up. Sasha successfully appealed to Lillian's desire to be seen as a trendsetter by arguing a loft wedding would be unique among her friends. In the end, Michelle got the wedding she wanted with full support of her Bankroller thanks to her Confidant.

A Word About Judgers

Many people can't avoid a Judger in their Wedding Committee. They can be tough, but they're part of your committee for a reason and you have to work with them. In these situations, the best defense is a good offense.

- You know their personalities. Try to anticipate what they care about ahead of time and prepare a respectful response.

- If possible, wait until you've done more homework on your vision and budget (discussed in chapters 3 and 4) before getting their input. The better armed you are with information to support your decision and alleviate their concerns, the greater likelihood you'll get them on your side.

REAL DEAL LIFE EXAMPLE #3:

Natalie

Natalie dreamed of a romantic destination wedding in the Caribbean. Her parents (both VIPs and Bankrollers) were concerned the additional travel expenses would make it too burdensome for their extended family to attend. Not to mention, navigating airports and a new location would be impossible for some beloved elderly relatives. For Natalie's parents, extended family was extremely important, and they wanted them to enjoy this milestone celebration.

As much as Natalie wanted her "dream wedding," she had to decide: did she want a tropical beach wedding, or did she want to be surrounded by three generations of family on her big day? Natalie compromised and got married in a nearby hotel with views overlooking the harbor. She worked with her florist to make the décor as tropical as possible inside a city hotel. They used orchids and palm leaves among other touches. In the end, the love and support of Natalie's large extended family proved more important than her original vision.

Unfortunately, some Judgers will never be satisfied. But if you take the time to consider their opinions, you may be able to persuade them to support your most important priorities. Ultimately, it's up to you how much importance you give their opinions.

The REAL DEAL About Wedding Committees

We've planned hundreds of weddings over the years and have seen this mistake again and again: couples or their families bulldoze ahead without talking to one another. The results are costly mistakes and painful misunderstandings such as venues that don't fit priorities, money spent in the wrong places, and couples with unrealistic expectations. As vendors, we're the ones left to troubleshoot and broker compromises. SMART wedding planning means communication. It means empowering yourself and managing your Wedding Committee from the start.

SIX TIPS FOR WORKING EFFECTIVELY WITH YOUR WEDDING COMMITTEE

1. **Plan ahead:** Before meeting with your Bankroller, talk with your partner about different options for size, location, and feel of your wedding. It helps to have a few ideas in mind, ranked in order of preference. You don't need to know the details or do any advance homework, but if your Bankroller is lukewarm on idea #1, they may love #2 or a combination of #2 and #3.

2. **Work together:** If you and your future spouse have more than one Confidant, divvy up any asks between them. Consider their individual personalities and skills when deciding who's better suited for each job. Maybe your Confidant cousin, who works as a therapist, is ideal to calm your anxious mother but isn't the right person to help pick out bridesmaid dresses.

REAL DEAL LIFE EXAMPLE #4:

Karina, Roberto, & Susannah

Karina was extremely close with her mother, Susannah. The two women agreed on almost everything. When Karina and Roberto got engaged, Susannah was thrilled. However, once Roberto's mother tried to get involved in the wedding planning, Susannah became a "Momzilla." Susannah vehemently objected to Roberto's mother's offer to throw the couple a small engagement party. She began speaking ill of Karina's future mother-in-law, creating tension between Karina and Roberto. Karina had never seen her mother behave so negatively.

As objective observers (and armchair psychologists), it appeared to us that Susannah was overly anxious about losing her special relationship with her daughter to Roberto's mother. Susannah may not have understood where her antagonism was coming from, but none-theless, her ardent refusal to include Roberto's mother in the wedding planning damaged her relationship with her future son-in-law. Our advice? When a "Zilla" rears its ugly head, stop and ask yourself, "What is this really about and how can I address the underlying cause?"

3. **Know your priorities:** Understand what's most important to you. Being clear in your mind what the nonnegotiables are makes it less likely you'll be talked into something you don't want.

4. **Pick your battles:** Picking your battles is a cliché but absolutely crucial when it comes to dealing with your Wedding Committee. If a VIP or Bankroller objects to one of your nonnegotiables, will you all survive the consequences? Is it worth it to dig in your heels? Are there alternatives you might consider?

5. **Document:** Keep a record of conversations and decisions to be sure everyone stays on the same page. For example, follow up the phone call with mom with an email that says, "We decided on the invitation with the pink flowers, and you will be placing the order by Friday."

6. **Be flexible:** It's a powerful tool to be able to compromise on things you don't feel strongly about. "Give and take" always puts you in a better position when fighting for a nonnegotiable. For example, maybe you agree to walk down the aisle to Wagner's "Bridal Chorus" because it's your father's wish, even though it's too traditional for your tastes. In exchange, you get an '80s cover band at the reception.

Summary

Your wedding day belongs to you and your family. Identifying your Wedding Committee is the first step in SMART wedding planning. Almost every major decision will be made with your committee's input. The Wedding Committee breaks down into three types of members:

> **The Bankrollers** – They're financing your wedding.
> **The VIPs** – Their opinions get high priority.
> **The Confidant** – They have your back, offer honest advice, and help you navigate the personalities involved in your wedding.

Anyone in these categories can be a Judger: Be aware of their personalities and be sure to communicate with them.

Establish the Rules of Engagement with your Bankrollers before committing to any decisions. Show respect and gratitude for their generosity. Determine your priorities and learn theirs. Uncover potential issues. Come to consensus.

Six Tips for Working Effectively with Your Wedding Committee:
1. Plan ahead
2. Work together
3. Know your priorities
4. Pick your battles
5. Document
6. Be flexible

CHAPTER

3

—— ◆ ——

CREATING YOUR
WEDDING

A generation ago, planning your wedding meant focusing on your gown, bridesmaid dresses, and flowers. If you were getting married then, you likely would have used the standard tableware, chairs, and linens offered by the venue. The menu options were limited, and it wasn't always the best meal. Concepts like farm-to-table and locally sourced didn't exist.

For the average couple, that was it. There was very little wedding personalization (except for matchbooks and cocktail napkins), and no one asked about your "wedding vision." In the pre-internet Dark Ages, anything beyond the standard wedding package took a herculean effort to plan: phone calls, snail mail, faxes, and multiple visits to vendors.

How Weddings Have Changed

THEN	NOW
Get engaged! Call everyone you know.	**Get engaged!** Call/text/selfie to family and friends, then post the news over social media.
Find Inspiration Go to bookstore, buy magazines.	**Find Inspiration** Join wedding websites, follow wedding bloggers, buy magazines and books. Create Pinterest page, tag favorite looks and ideas, follow celebrities and other fashion trends.
Wedding Party Ask close friends and family to be in your wedding party.	**Wedding Party** Create wedding party "proposals" with elaborate and customized gifts that say things like, "Will you be my bridesmaid?" or "I can't say I do without you!"

THEN	NOW
Research Make phone calls to learn about venue and vendors.	**Research** Gather information online mostly using mobile devices.
Venues Get list of area venues from bridal magazines or friends/family. Visit venues in person (houses of worship, reception halls, hotels).	**Venues** Explore different venue ideas (from traditional to unconventional) online. Tour virtually to narrow down options. Follow venues on social media. Read reviews, search for images online, then visit a few venues in person.
Attend wedding expos Attend large events with hundreds of vendors.	**Attend wedding expos** Attend more intimate events like unique venue open houses with preferred vendors or entertainment showcases to pick a band or DJ.
Menu Chicken, Fish, Beef	**Menu** Multicourse meals, food trucks, raw bars, cheese bars, signature cocktails, late-night snacks, vegan/paleo/food allergies, donut wall, miniature foods

THEN	NOW
Décor Local flowers, tiered cake, basic invitations, monogrammed cocktail napkins and matchbooks	**Décor** Custom invitations, worldwide flowers, signature drinks, dancefloor monograms, tablecloths in any color and fabric, lounges, installations, soft lighting options
Planning Phone, fax, wedding binder, handwritten checklists	**Planning** Email, texts, video conferencing, online planning apps. Pinterest, Instagram, Etsy Hire a planner.
Registry Register at department stores.	**Registry** Online registries
Entertainment DJ, band, string quartet, harpist	**Entertainment** DJ, band, quartet, photo booth, outdoor and indoor games (corn hole, chess), ballet or other professional performances (rap, A capella groups, aerialists), video photo booth, cigar rolling, "make your own" activities (candy/ice cream)

THEN	NOW
Event Rehearsal dinner Wedding ceremony Reception	**Event** Wedding Weekend Experience (rehearsal dinner, after party, tour buses, golfing expeditions, spa treatments, next-day farewell brunch)
Extras Guest book	**Extras** Guest sign-in activities (sign the poster, message in bottle, wishing tree) Greeting bags for out-of-town guests with snacks, water, and information about the area On-site childcare Pets in photos and ceremony
Documenting the Day Photographer Videographer	**Documenting the Day** Photographer—engagement sessions, rehearsal dinner, getting ready, first look, and wedding day photos Videographer—drones, same-day edits, customized movies Photo booths, video maps, live-streaming, GIF booths, hashtags

The opportunities to personalize every aspect of your wedding are mind-boggling. Practically anything you can imagine can be ordered online, from custom monogrammed aisle runners to cake toppers created in the happy couple's image. Your wedding is no longer limited by what's available in your area.

You'd think access to "anything you want" would make it easier to realize your wedding vision, but in fact, it can make it more difficult. Too many choices can lead to decision fatigue, especially when you haven't narrowed down your ideas. Learning how to develop a vision will make decision-making easier in the long run.

Three Steps To Creating Your Wedding Vision

We can't help you pick your colors or design elements (unless you hire us), but we can demystify the process of bringing your wedding vision to life. There's no magic involved. It comes down to three steps:

1. **Approach:** Decide which approach you'll choose for your wedding.

2. **Vision:** Determine your vision for the overall look, feel, and experience you want to create.

3. **Show & Tell:** Convey your vision to those who need to know.

APPROACH

There are several general approaches in wedding planning. Each one can produce a spectacular event. Here's a breakdown:

Themed weddings: This is exactly what it sounds like: a wedding inspired by a distinctive motif or theme. A themed wedding makes a very specific statement that's immediately clear to anyone who attends. Guests may even partake in the theme and dress accordingly. Some examples include:

  o Movie or TV series – Star Trek, Game of Thrones, Classic Hollywood

o Fashion, Music, and Culture—Vintage, Goth, Masquerade, Halloween, Elvis
o Location—Beach, Mountain, Barn
o Hobbies—Travel, Reading, Birdwatching

Designed weddings: Some couples don't have a particular theme in mind; they simply want a beautiful, well-produced wedding. In a designed wedding, the flowers, décor, and other elements complement the venue and bring the couple's aesthetic to fruition, creating a memorable and meaningful day.

Personalized weddings: Personalized weddings are about showcasing the couple's personality, style, values, and beliefs. These weddings can be beautifully designed or even inspired by a theme, but it's more about making the wedding day unique—touches like signature drinks, sentimental décor or favors, special additions to the ceremony, entertainment, and family traditions.

Branded weddings: Branded weddings are the next stage in the evolution of personalized weddings. Couples work with professional designers and branding experts to deliver an experience that not only reflects who they are, but also builds excitement and shares their story with their guests. It's more than creating a logo or a signature drink, though those are two great ways to personalize a wedding. It involves thinking strategically about the big picture and how all the components—venue, ceremony, food, beverage, design, entertainment, logistics, wedding website, social media, and everything else—are rendered in a consistent and cohesive style so the couple's visual narrative is realized.

These are not rigid categories. A couple often chooses to personalize or add branding elements to their themed wedding. Overlap is common. These distinctions are not intended to tie your hands, but rather encourage you to take a step back and look at the overall direction you're heading. Does it feel right? The clearer your approach, the easier it becomes to cut through the noise and make the best decisions. It's your roadmap to the wedding you desire.

The clearer your
Wedding Vision
Statement, the better
your vendors can help
you realize that vision
and avoid costly
mistakes down
the road.

VISION

People often confuse vision with style, but in the wedding world, they are not the same thing. Style is associated with how things look; for example, room décor and wedding attire. While these are important in shaping the vision, they're just a part of it. Vision is more comprehensive—it's the overall look, feel, and experience you want to create. Think of the first impression you want your guests to feel when they walk into the venue. Think about the music playing (smooth jazz or a live acoustic guitarist), the lighting (soft romantic or bold and blue), the smells (flowers or food) and the overall ambiance. Do you want it to feel romantic and elegant? Or do you want a major WOW factor right when guests walk in? Keep in mind this can change as the night goes on: the music can change, the lighting can change, and you can even change clothes as the party starts to get going and the dance floor fills up!

We find most couples have some idea of what they want in the beginning, but those ideas are vague and unstructured. They're like a half-baked cake: the main ingredients are there, but it needs more work to make it delicious (and edible!).

It's not uncommon for the one partner to have one vision in mind, while the other partner has another. Things get complicated quickly. You don't need to figure out every detail right away. Your vision will naturally be refined over time as you work with vendors. However, it's crucial to come to an agreement with your partner and Bankrollers on the general direction before you start planning. And by "general direction," we mean writing a wedding vision statement that everyone is on board with. This step is crucial.

CREATING YOUR WEDDING VISION STATEMENT

You may already know what you like, but writing those thoughts down in a concise vision statement that satisfies both you and your partner is the best way to solidify your ideas. This next exercise is an excellent way to discover your preferences and compare them with your partner's. When you've completed this, writing a Wedding Vision Statement you both love will be easy. This is meant to be simple and fun. It's basically a matter of filling in the blanks. We'll walk you through it.

Complete the "Create Your Wedding Vision" worksheet.

You and your partner should each do the worksheet separately. Don't look at what your partner writes. The goal is to dig deep within yourself to see what you want without anyone else's influence. We give you suggestions for descriptive words, but write whatever you want.

SETTING

What's your ideal location?

(You have ideas for your location based on your initial budget research, but this is the time to make sure the type of venue you've identified is the best fit for your vision.)

Ideas/Suggestions
city, beach, barn, ballroom, backyard, country club, brewery, vineyard/ winery, restaurant, museum, library, function hall, religious institution, raw/industrial space, tent, historic mansion, outdoor/nature, city hall

_____

_____

_____

_____

_____

_____

_____

_____

What season or time of year would you like to get married?

winter, spring, summer, fall, holiday

_____

What time of day do you want?

morning, afternoon, evening, night

_____

SETTING

WORKSHEET FOR YOUR PARTNER

What's your ideal location?

(You have ideas for your location
based on your initial budget research,
but this is the time to make sure the
type of venue you've identified is the
best fit for your vision.)

Ideas/Suggestions
*city, beach, barn, ballroom, backyard,
country club, brewery, vineyard/
winery, restaurant, museum, library,
function hall, religious institution,
raw/industrial space, tent, historic
mansion, outdoor/nature, city hall*

_____

_____

_____

_____

_____

_____

_____

**What season or time of year
would you like to get married?**

winter, spring, summer, fall, holiday

_____

What time of day do you want?

morning, afternoon, evening, night

_____

PERSONALITY AND STYLE

What is your individual style/ personality?

casual, glitzy, formal, clean, minimalist, rustic, goth, artistic, bohemian-chic, glamorous, whimsical, preppy, sleek, elegant, hip-hop, earthy, designer, edgy, comfortable, athletic-sporty, classic, modern, biker, outdoorsy, trendy, feminine, romantic, masculine, flamboyant, high-end, traditional

How would you describe your style/ personality as a couple?

casual, glitzy, formal, clean, minimalist, rustic, goth, artistic, bohemian-chic, glamorous, whimsical, preppy, sleek, elegant, hip-hop, earthy, designer, edgy, comfortable, athletic-sporty, classic, modern, biker, outdoorsy, trendy, feminine, romantic, masculine, flamboyant, high-end, traditional

What type of mood do you want to evoke?

European/cosmopolitan, steampunk, grunge, street style/urban, flashy, private, intimate, grand, romantic, cozy, vintage, elegant, fun, celebratory, exciting, inspiring, funny, religious, intellectual, nostalgic, traditional, sentimental, passionate, adventurous, tender, fairy tale, charming, enchanting, exotic, fantasy

PERSONALITY AND STYLE WORSHEET FOR YOUR PARTNER

What is your individual style/ personality?

casual, glitzy, formal, clean, minimalist, rustic, goth, artistic, bohemian-chic, glamorous, whimsical, preppy, sleek, elegant, hip-hop, earthy, designer, edgy, comfortable, athletic-sporty, classic, modern, biker, outdoorsy, trendy, feminine, romantic, masculine, flamboyant, high-end, traditional

How would you describe your style/ personality as a couple?

casual, glitzy, formal, clean, minimalist, rustic, goth, artistic, bohemian-chic, glamorous, whimsical, preppy, sleek, elegant, hip-hop, earthy, designer, edgy, comfortable, athletic-sporty, classic, modern, biker, outdoorsy, trendy, feminine, romantic, masculine, flamboyant, high-end, traditional

What type of mood do you want to evoke?

European/cosmopolitan, steampunk, grunge, street style/urban, flashy, private, intimate, grand, romantic, cozy, vintage, elegant, fun, celebratory, exciting, inspiring, funny, religious, intellectual, nostalgic, traditional, sentimental, passionate, adventurous, tender, fairy tale, charming, enchanting, exotic, fantasy

EXPERIENCE

What do you want your guests to say about your wedding and their experience afterwards?

"This wedding perfectly reflected who the couple is."

"We danced all night. The music was amazing. It was the best party we've ever been to."

"It was the most stunning wedding I've ever seen."

"The food was outstanding. Everything was cooked to perfection."

"They really went out of their way to make sure we had a good time."

_____

_____

_____

_____

_____

_____

What are the 1-3 things you saw at another wedding or event that you'd LOVE to do at yours?

_____

_____

_____

_____

What are the 1-3 things you saw at another wedding or event that you want to AVOID at all costs?

_____

_____

_____

_____

What are your style and experience must-haves?

A lounge area for my friends to hang out, Comfort, Lots of candles, Sustainable living, A view of the mountains, A dramatic entrance, Peonies, No kids, Gluten-free menu, Eight-piece band

_____

_____

_____

EXPERIENCE   WORSHEET FOR YOUR PARTNER

What do you want your guests to say about your wedding and their experience afterwards?

"This wedding perfectly reflected who the couple is."

"We danced all night. The music was amazing. It was the best party we've ever been to."

"It was the most stunning wedding I've ever seen."

"The food was outstanding. Everything was cooked to perfection."

"They really went out of their way to make sure we had a good time."

_____

_____

_____

_____

_____

_____

_____

_____

_____

What are the 1-3 things you saw at another wedding or event that you'd LOVE to do at yours?

_____

_____

_____

_____

What are the 1-3 things you saw at another wedding or event that you want to AVOID at all costs?

_____

_____

_____

_____

What are your style and experience must-haves?

A lounge area for my friends to hang out, Comfort, Lots of candles, Sustainable living, A view of the mountains, A dramatic entrance, Peonies, No kids, Gluten-free menu, Eight-piece band

_____

_____

_____

_____

45

VALUES AND INTERESTS

**What's important to you at
your wedding?**

Honoring tradition and family

Ensuring guests have fun

*Making a statement about our
lifestyle or things we believe in*

High quality, locally sourced food

Making sure it's a beautiful day

*Making sure our religious or
cultural beliefs are expressed*

_____

_____

_____

_____

_____

_____

_____

_____

_____

**What is it that you have most in
common together or that connects
you as a couple?**

*Our love of our dogs/animals and
the things we do with them*

*Our love of our family traditions
and culture/religion*

*We're foodies and love to try
different restaurants or bars.*

*Our friends and social scene are a
huge part of our life, and we're always
attending or hosting parties.*

_____

_____

_____

_____

_____

_____

_____

_____

VALUES AND INTERESTS   WORKSHEET FOR YOUR PARTNER

**What's important to you at
your wedding?**

Honoring tradition and family

Ensuring guests have fun

*Making a statement about our
lifestyle or things we believe in*

High quality, locally sourced food

Making sure it's a beautiful day

*Making sure our religious or
cultural beliefs are expressed*

_____

_____

_____

_____

_____

_____

_____

_____

_____

_____

**What is it that you have most in
common together or that connects
you as a couple?**

*Our love of our dogs/animals and
the things we do with them*

*Our love of our family traditions
and culture/religion*

*We're foodies and love to try
different restaurants or bars.*

*Our friends and social scene are a
huge part of our life, and we're always
attending or hosting parties.*

_____

_____

_____

_____

_____

_____

_____

_____

_____

_____

Once you complete the worksheet, you and your partner can:

Compare notes: Share your worksheets with each other. Where do you and your partner align and where do you differ? This is when you'll have a heart-to-heart about what matters and your must-haves. You may or may not be surprised. Many people end up discussing who they are as a couple and as individuals. This is an important conversation to have, so give it the time it deserves. Maybe the conversation takes place over a few days so you can consider your partner's point of view. It may seem like a therapy session, but now is the time to figure out where you're both on the same page and where you have to compromise.

Pick your top descriptors: In each category (setting, personality and style, experience, values and interests), pick the top one or two descriptors you both agree upon. You may be required to give up something in order to get something else. Remember, you're creating a wedding vision statement that represents both of you.

Write your Wedding Vision Statement: Use your top descriptors to fill out our Wedding Vision Template. That's it! That's your Wedding Vision Statement. Read it over. Fine-tune it as you see fit. How does your gut feel when you read it? Go through a few versions if necessary until it feels absolutely authentic to you and your partner. This paragraph should encapsulate the look, feel, and experience you want to create—this is your roadmap to your wedding vision!

Share your Wedding Vision Statement with your Wedding Committee: It's crucial to share your wedding vision with your Bankroller(s), VIPs, and even Confidants, if you like. If they raise any issues, it's best to be aware of them before you begin creating your budget and looking for vendors. After you've shared your statement, decide if you need to make adjustments. Keep working on it if necessary. Make certain your Wedding Vision Statement is one everyone is on board with. You're going to use this statement to shape your entire wedding.

WEDDING VISION STATEMENT TEMPLATE

We want a (season) wedding in the (PLACE - *mountains, beach, city, etc.*). Our wedding style will be (STYLE - *bohemian, classic, trendy, etc.*), and we'd like the wedding to evoke our sense of (NOUN - *whimsy, humor, sophistication, etc.*). We want to make sure the wedding high-lights how much we love (NOUN - *nature, books, movies, etc.*). We'd like (SPECIAL REQUESTS HERE - *children welcome, no cameras, dramatic entrance, etc.*). Our must-haves include: (MUST-HAVES - *can be anything you absolutely MUST HAVE*).

Here are a few example wedding vision statements to get you started:

We want a Saturday night summer wedding in an industrial raw space. Our wedding style will be nontraditional and urban, and we'd like the wedding to feel contemporary and hip. We want to make sure the wedding highlights how much we love to dance and make sure our friends have a great time. We'd like a lounge area for friends and family and lots of candles/mood lighting—we want it to feel like a cool night-club. Our must-haves include fantastic music and lighting effects.

We want a spring wedding in a country club or hotel. Our wedding style will be elegant and classic, and we'd like the wedding to evoke our sense of sophistication and romance. We want to make sure the wedding highlights how much we love our family and tradition. We'd like a dra-matic entrance and want guests to contribute to a 10-year anniversary message-in-a-bottle keepsake. Our must-haves include beautiful center-pieces, gourmet food, and top-shelf liquor.

We want a fall wedding in the countryside. Our wedding style will be bohemian-chic glamping, and we'd like the wedding to evoke our sense of whimsy. We want to make sure the wedding highlights how much we love nature. We'd like folks to feel welcome to bring their dogs and young chil-dren. Our must-haves include a beautiful rustic-chic venue with gorgeous views and to include our dogs in the ceremony.

SHOW & TELL

If you can't get enough of Pinterest, you're going to love this part. Even if you don't, you'll be thankful you completed this step. A picture is worth a thousand words when you're talking to vendors. It's time to create a visual representation of your Wedding Vision Statement.

You've already created the written description—now you're simply choosing images to go with your words. Type words from your Wedding Vision Statement into search engines to find inspiration. Pinterest is an excellent way to collect images, but there are other ways to do this: rip pages from magazines, take screenshots, bookmark a bunch of photos. How you collect pictures is up to you; just make them easy to access. In essence, you're creating a "portfolio" of your vision. To ensure your portfolio does its intended job, we recommend including at least three images per category. Categories can include things like venue, table-scapes, flowers, dresses, and décor.

During this process, you may find a lot of images you love that have nothing to do with your Wedding Vision Statement. We strongly suggest you ignore them or put them aside. Please don't include them in your portfolio. It will be confusing to your vendors. Only collect images that relate to your vision statement.

Once you're finished, this portfolio becomes your wedding vision. How do you feel when you look at it? Joyful? Excited? If you feel indifferent or just meh, don't ignore those feelings! Take a deep breath and pause. We want you to be happy with the direction you're heading. This is your wedding. Does your Wedding Vision Statement truly reflect your desires? Have you compromised so much there's not enough of "you" in your wedding vision? If this is where you are, have a heart-to-heart with your partner, Bankroller, and VIPs. Get your Confidant's opinion. The good news is, if you've been following our steps, you haven't committed to anything yet, so you can course-correct as necessary.

Why is going through this "Approach, Vision, Show & Tell" exercise worth your time? It's the exact process used by the best wedding planners and branding experts in the business. They ask these same questions and collect images to accurately articulate the mood, feeling, and experience you want to create. They get a sense of you and your partner's personalities, how you met, what you care about, even the jokes you share. All these pieces of information come together to tell a story—*your* story. When you say you'd like a romantic or casual wedding, they put those words into the context of who you are. From there, it becomes easier to define your style and realize your vision. If you don't anticipate hiring a planner or branding professional, then creating this portfolio is a must-have tool for developing your vision on your own. It will be invaluable to you in three important ways:

Selecting the right vendors: Before meeting with a potential vendor, check to see if your portfolio is aesthetically similar to a vendor's online portfolio or gallery. For example, if you peruse a photographer's website and see mostly formal, posed groupings and your portfolio shows natural, documentary-style pictures, it may not be the best match. Likewise, when you check out a potential florist's Instagram feed and find nothing but hotel ballrooms when you're planning a barn wedding with a rustic theme, maybe you need to keep looking.

Once you meet with prospective vendors, your portfolio is a visual shortcut. Instead of only using words to describe what you want, the portfolio paints a picture. Now you can focus on what the vendor has to say. Do they understand what you're going for? Do they have thoughtful suggestions for how to build upon your vision? Do you feel this is someone you could work with on a personal level?

Having a portfolio puts you ahead of the game when determining whether a vendor is a good fit. We suggest comparing your portfolio to the venue you're considering as well. Does it match? If not, keep looking. Your venue is a vendor too.

Staying within your vision and budget: It's much easier to stick to a budget when you're designing with a clear vision in mind. Every decision you make, from the type of flowers to the music to the food, needs to answer the questions: Does it reflect your vision? Is it necessary? Can you do it another way? When you know what you want, saying no becomes infinitely easier. It's always the couples that lack focus who end up going off track and buying things they don't need. We'll talk about this more in the next chapter on building your REAL DEAL budget. But for now, know your portfolio is your touchstone for every decision you make.

Avoiding misunderstandings and mistakes: Understand that descriptive words are subjective. Be sure you clarify with your vendors when describing a vision. Your idea of glamour may be vastly different than your florist's. Don't assume saying, "I want glamour," is enough. You may be thinking *The Great Gatsby* while your florist is thinking Hollywood chic. Having a portfolio is an excellent communication tool. It reduces errors, misunderstandings, and "back and forth." It gets you where you want to go quickly.

Summary

The wedding industry offers more options for creating a customized wedding than ever before. The sheer number of choices is overwhelming. We recommend a three-step process to transform the hazy images in your head into a concrete wedding vision.

1. **Approach:** Decide on a themed, designed, personalized, or branded wedding—or some combination of each.

2. **Vision:** You and your partner each fill out the wedding vision worksheet separately. Discuss your answers and see where you agree and differ. Then write your joint Wedding Vision Statement using our Wedding Vision Template paragraph. Refine it until it perfectly reflects your vision. Share it with your Wedding Committee. Make sure everyone is on board.

3. **Show & Tell:** Collect images that accurately depict your Wedding Vision Statement and create a portfolio. This becomes the visual representation of your wedding vision. You should feel joy when you look at your portfolio. If not, press the pause button and determine where you went off track. You'll use this tool with your vendors and Wedding Committee in the planning process.

**Your wedding vision portfolio
is an invaluable tool to help you:**

1. Select your vendors
2. Stay true to your vision and your budget
3. Avoid misunderstandings and mistakes

CHAPTER

4

◆

BUILDING YOUR
REAL DEAL

Budget

Time To Talk Money

Now that you've identified your Wedding Committee and created your wedding vision, you need to figure out how much it's all going to cost. It's time to calculate your REAL DEAL Wedding Budget.

You probably have a general idea of how much money you have to spend after consulting with your Bankroller and factoring in your own financial situation. But here's the tricky part—that number is simply your starting point. You now need to make sure the funds available align with your vision. If they don't, you can make some adjustments before you start spending money and signing contracts. That's what this chapter is about: comprehending and calculating (two of the Three Cs from chapter 1) wedding expenses and learning how to build a realistic budget that can make your wedding vision come to fruition.

Setting and sticking to a budget is the most stressful part of wedding planning. Budgeting, like tracking household expenses or planning for retirement, is just one of those things people hate to do and tend to avoid.[5] In our experience, newly engaged couples are no different. Nearly 50% of couples exceed their intended wedding budgets[6], and we don't want that to happen to you.

Going over budget doesn't necessarily mean these couples are not accurately informed. It takes very little effort to uncover the latest wedding cost data and many couples have done some amount of research. A few Google searches can reveal the average cost of a wedding across different regions, right down to the ZIP code. But once couples start talking to vendors, a vastly different reality begins to emerge. The difference between the dollar amount in their heads and the dollar amount they *actually* need to achieve their vision can be huge. We like to call this the "Wedding Budget Knowledge Gap."

This gap can be very wide and a source of stress and worry. We meet so many frustrated couples and families who have blown their budgets or

---

[5] Dennis Jacobe, "One in Three Americans Prepare a Detailed Household Budget," June 2, 2013, https://news.gallup.com/poll/162872/one-three-americans-prepare-detailed-household-budget.aspx.

[6] Kim Forrest, "More Couples Than You Think Go Over Their Wedding Budget (and Here's How Much They Overspend)," March 3, 2022, https://www.theknot.com/content/how-many-couples-spend-over-budget

are on their way to doing so. Often, they don't realize the consequences of their choices until it's too late.

Are we suggesting you have to spend a large amount of money to get what you want? Well, that depends on what you want. What we're *really* saying is this: While some wedding expenses can't be predicted, the *majority* can be understood and managed.

We know money is not everyone's favorite topic, and many are uncomfortable talking about it. But it's crucial to communicate and think openly about money during the wedding planning process.

You may be asking yourself if it's really worth it to spend all this money on a wedding. There are only so many milestones in life: births, christenings, bar and bat mitzvahs, quinceañeras, graduations, weddings. These are momentous occasions, and they should be celebrated. That's why there are so many rituals attached to them. We believe it's never a waste of money to bring people together in joy and create memories. That's what life is about. But we also feel strongly that you need to know what you're getting into, so you can make the best choices.

There's no way around it; it's going to cost money. And we're here to help you get real about what things cost, what you can afford, and how you can create and stick to a budget. We'll guide you on how to manage or adjust your priorities to achieve the most important aspects of your wedding vision. The lessons here apply to every budget. A well-planned wedding, regardless of whether it's 20 people at a backyard barbeque or 300 people in a formal ballroom, is a wonderful celebration.

REAL DEAL FACT 9

Weddings are expensive. It costs money to celebrate with 100 or 200 of your closest family and friends if you want to feed them, serve them drinks, and make it all look festive. You'll likely be hiring vendors to make floral bouquets, bake a cake, and take photos— all of this costs money.

Creating A Realistic Budget And Sticking To It

It's important to understand the challenges you're up against when planning your wedding. The impact of social media on the wedding industry has been transformational. It's also a primary reason couples find it so hard to create a realistic and affordable budget. In the "old days" (20-plus years ago), couples relied on friends and family for recommendations, looked to wedding magazines for inspiration, and followed the customs that worked in their community, religion, or social group. They relied on the same vendors who offered the same services and products to everyone else in that community. As a result, costs were more predictable.

Today's couples have been exposed to an entirely new world. In the United States, the average age of first marriage is 28 for women and 30 for men.[7] Couples are older and savvier when they get married than in previous generations. They pin, tag, favorite, rank, follow, and share wedding ideas anytime, anywhere. They find inspiration everywhere. They tap into online communities, check out other couples (including celebrities), and explore ideas through social media.

What does all this have to do with your budget? A lot. It means that practically anything you can imagine is possible. The ability to find and source ideas is instantaneous and limitless. Couples expect more from their weddings, and the industry has evolved to serve their every whim and desire. This has forced traditional wedding vendors to improve their game to face new competition.

The online world has not only changed wedding planning, it's driving many trends impacting your ability to create a realistic budget.

---

[7] Kim Forrest, "More Couples Than You Think Go Over Their Wedding Budget (and Here's How Much They Overspend)," March 3, 2022, https://www.theknot.com/content/how-many-couples-spend-over-budget

A wedding is more than an event: Couples increasingly view their wedding as a meaningful milestone in "their story." It's more than just a six-hour party; it's about delivering an experience that starts long before the wedding day. Couples want their wedding to reflect their backgrounds and their personalities. It's their opportunity to put their stamp on the world. They want family and friends to join them on their journey—to experience a little slice of their lives together. This "wedding experience" mindset is the defining difference between current weddings and those of older generations.

More and more options: It's faster and easier to get anything you want from anywhere in the world. Take flowers for example. With a simple email, your florist can launch a shipment of the best possible hydrangeas cut from a field in Colombia and delivered to their store. Or if your priority is to support local businesses, they can source seasonal flowers directly from a local organic farm. Even if you're looking to have a no-frills wedding, nothing is simple anymore. Every item you select offers a plethora of micro choices. Twenty years ago, the question was, "What napkin color would you like?" Now, you're not only selecting napkin color, you're also choosing fabric, texture, and size among a sea of alternatives. You can choose from any number of chair styles. There are literally hundreds of lighting options to create just the right mood at the exact right moment. All these choices individually are relatively affordable, but when you add them together, it can put you over your budget.

Greater personalization: With so many options, weddings have an unprecedented level of creativity and personalization. Couples are constantly discovering new ideas. They're adding personal touches with custom monograms, food trucks, beer gardens, drone photography, video mapping, signature drinks—the list goes on and the possibilities are endless. Couples are honoring each other in artistic and innovative ways, reinventing what it means to get married.

When you consider how much weddings (and society) have transformed in a single generation, it's no wonder weddings have become so costly. It's why expectations often don't align with reality. It always costs more than you think it will. Does that mean you have to go into debt to have the wedding you desire? No. But you do have to start with an accurate budget that takes into account what your wedding will truly cost you.

Building Your REAL DEAL Wedding Budget

There's a right way to create a budget and several wrong ways. Let's start with what you shouldn't do.

THE WRONG WAYS

- Plug the amount you have to spend into an online wedding budget-calculator, see how it allocates the total, and then try to find vendors who will fit that price point. The problem with this method is that the breakdown may work mathematically (50% for food, 10% for flowers, etc.), but it might not take into consideration the specifics of your situation. For example, you may have 200 people on the guest list, and 50% of your budget won't even cover a sandwich and soda per person. Or you may have an idea for very lavish centerpieces that will exceed 10% of total costs. Every wedding is different—hence, every wedding budget must be unique.

- Choose options without considering them in the context of your wedding as whole. Let's say you know you want to get married in a beautiful downtown hotel. You visit a number of options, find the perfect ballroom, and book it. Whoa! Now you've done it. This means your entire budget is based on the cost of your venue—not your wedding. The venue and food combined is likely to be your single largest expense, but there are many other factors you should consider. This misguided approach inevitably leads to the phenomenon we call being "venue poor" (see REAL DEAL Life Example #5: Rachel).

- Start spending money and hope your total budget will cover everything. Most often the money is gone before all your vendors are booked. We can't tell you how many times Jeri has heard, "We don't have money left for the flowers because we've already spent our entire budget."

THE RIGHT WAY

Before booking any vendors, be sure to research the 10 vendor categories most often hired for weddings to get an accurate and informed picture of what your wedding will truly cost. This is the comprehension part of the Three Cs: You need to understand everything that's involved in a wedding budget before you begin to spend money.

THE FIVE-STEP METHOD FOR BUILDING YOUR REAL DEAL WEDDING BUDGET

Your objective is to determine what the wedding you want is likely to cost. This is a fact-finding mission, and it requires work on your part. Do you recall us saying in the introduction that planning a wedding can be as time consuming as a second job? Well, this is why. But consider this: You're about to spend a large sum of money. Would you spend money building a house or buying a car without educating yourself first? We hope not. The same rules apply here.

We realize, of course, not everyone has the time or inclination to do the comprehensive research. This is one of the biggest reasons people hire wedding planners. (We'll get into the role of wedding planners more in chapter 6.) A good wedding planner knows your local market, the vendors, and what things cost. Another benefit is that they can leverage their relationships with vendors to work in your favor. Some planners might be willing to consult with you just about budget, but if you're not using a planner, our five-step method will give you the information you need to create a realistic budget. If you skip this part, don't be surprised when you've reached your budget's limit before you've hired all your vendors.

On average, most people hire 10 vendors to pull off their wedding. This process gives you the tools to arrive at an accurate estimate for each one of those vendors.

1. **Look at the big picture first and don't worry about wedding time-tables yet:** You've probably heard somewhere along the way: "Book your venue a year in advance," "Talk to the florists six months before," or "Secure your stylist three months out." There's nothing inherently wrong with this advice, but you'll never be able to create a realistic budget and stick to it if you spend large portions of your overall budget upfront on some vendors while waiting months before talking to others. We've seen this approach and it leads to surprises and disappointments. Make it your goal to contact every vendor you think you'll need for price quotes at the beginning of the process. This is very important. You're not hiring everyone right away, but you need to know all of the estimated costs in order to see the big picture.

2. **Find your key vendors:** On the next page is a list of the top 10 types of vendors most people hire for weddings. These are the most common categories, but often people use more. We have a list for those "extra" vendors a little later in the chapter. If you want the most accurate estimate of what each vendor costs, consider contacting three vendors in each category—that's 30 vendors total! Yep, it sounds like a lot. However, with the help of the internet and by utilizing our REAL DEAL email script, you can get a lot of information quickly and efficiently. Still, if this seems like too much work, contact at least one of each vendor in a price range that appeals to you (high-end, mid-range, or budget). Look at your priorities and must-haves from your Wedding Vision Statement for guidance. If jaw-dropping centerpieces and décor are important to you, reach out to a florist known for their elaborate work. Even if your best friend says, "Use my florist. She was so reasonable and did a fantastic job," we still recommend researching other vendors. Your friend's vision and priorities might have been different from yours. The more effort you put in here, the more accurate your budget will be.

TOP 10 CATEGORIES OF WEDDING VENDORS

1. **Wedding planner**

2. **Reception venue**
   including food beverage

3. **Caterer**
   if venue does not provide food/ beverage

4. **Florist**

5. **Photographer**

6. **Videographer**

7. **Entertainment**
   DJ, band, musicians, etc.

8. **Stationery**
   invitations, placecards, menus, etc.

9. **Makeup/hair stylist**

10. **Cake baker**

Note: Wedding attire is not technically a vendor category, but it's a big budget expense that we address later in the chapter.

HOW TO FIND THESE VENDORS

This is a fact-finding mission, not necessarily your final selections. You're simply trying to get an idea of current rates in your area for the vendors that appeal to you. We go into detail about the vendor hiring process in chapter 6, "Assembling Your Vendor Team."

• Pick a category, such as photographer, DJ, florist, etc., from the Top 10 Types of Wedding Vendors list to the left.

• Search the internet for the category of vendor you're looking for in your area or near your venue. For example, if you're looking for Boston-area photographers, enter "Boston wedding photographers" into the search box. Also, be sure to check out well-known websites that offer reviews and include lists of vendors in your geographic location. Many venues also have a preferred vendor list. When looking at venue websites or social media, see whether they have vendors who have worked in their space and that match your vision/aesthetic.

• Choose three vendors (or at least one) from that category that appealed to you based on a quick review of their online information. Go with your first impressions.

• If you're looking at options on a website or directory where vendors are categorized by price point, pick one from each price category. However, don't make assumptions of how expensive or inexpensive vendors might be based on those dollar signs alone. They're not always accurate, and cost is always relative. It's worth reaching out to folks at each price level to get a good sense of the range of what things cost.

• Create a list of vendors to contact for each category, being sure to include the email address you plan to use to reach out to them.

3. **Contact each vendor on your list using our REAL DEAL email script:** By using the REAL DEAL email script, you'll be able to quickly reach all the vendors you've identified, get the information you need to build an accurate budget, and eliminate the vendors you absolutely don't want to work with. (These are the ones that don't respond to your message or simply don't seem to be on the same wavelength as you.)

Note: Some vendors may have pricing or packages listed on their websites, so you won't have to reach out in those cases (fewer emails to send on your part—look how easy!). However, consider the prices listed on a website as a base price only. The prices increase rather quickly when you add individual options to standard packages.

It's important to remember that this part of the vendor search is a *fact-finding mission* only. You are looking to get *quick price estimates* from each vendor based on the information you provide; you are *not* negotiating or committing yourself to any vendor. You also don't need to disclose any information about how much money you have to spend— you're simply gathering information necessary to build your budget.

Using this script is one of our favorite pieces of REAL DEAL wedding advice. It's what we'd do in your shoes to get the most accurate information out of vendors. Many vendors will reply back with everything you need in an email. Some might want to jump on the phone for a few minutes to ask additional questions. If someone wants to talk with you, it means they're interested in your business and want to help, so it's worth taking the time. What you learn in those few minutes can put you leaps and bounds ahead of the game as an educated wedding consumer.

If you don't hear back from a vendor within one to two business days, scratch them off your list and email another vendor in that category. Our email template makes it easy to reach out to people quickly. The goal is to get at least one quote per category, but aim for three. Before you know it, you'll have all the information you need to create a realistic budget. And guess what? This initial work will make you extremely knowledgeable, and the rest of your wedding planning will be so much easier.

THE REAL DEAL EMAIL SCRIPT

To: **Vendor**

Subject: **Wedding information needed**

Hello [Vendor],
I'm in the beginning stages of planning my wedding, and I'm working on building an accurate budget. I'm contacting you because I found you [online, through a friend, or however you learned about them] and I like what I see on [your website or their other social media].

Here's what I know so far about my wedding: [Tell the vendor as much information as you know at this time from the list below.]
• Wedding date, month, season, or day of the week you're thinking
• Ceremony location you envision
• Type of reception locations you're looking at (i.e., hotel, country club, country setting, by the ocean, etc.) or a specific place if you have one in mind
• Approximate number of guests
• Number of people in the wedding party for both sides. Not every vendor needs this information, but the florist, hair, and makeup vendors will need to know.
• Other information you may want to share that is applicable to that vendor. For example, "I want peonies everywhere" (florist); "We're having an Elvis-themed wedding" (cake baker); "We'd like to have a flash mob dance" (DJ). These details give the vendor a sense of the style and scale of your wedding and help them provide you with the most appropriate cost and service options.

Approximately how much money can I expect to spend with you for my wedding? I'm interested in knowing a base price for a starting package as well as additional upgrades and options.

Please indicate whether your price includes all taxes and fees or if that will be additional. Finally, please tell me if there's anything else I should know when hiring a [the type of vendor].

Thank you so much for your help!
Sincerely,
[Your Name—aka smart person planning a wedding]

4. **Add up your estimates—then pad the total because it's going to cost more!** Once you've collected all your estimates, tally them up. Consider what's most important to you. If you love beautiful flowers or want an amazing venue, then use the highest price estimate for that category to factor into your budget. Otherwise, take the midrange estimate for each vendor category and add them up. The resulting number is your vendor total—but still not your total budget! You need to pad your total by at least 20%, at a minimum. Some people pad their total by 30 to 40%. This is important because it leaves room for all the "surprises" and "must-haves" you won't discover until later down the road. (Chapter 6 gives you a list of some common unexpected costs.) These unexpected expenses are a basic fact of wedding planning. It's going to cost more than you think. It always does. So be smart—prepare by building a cushion into your budget.

5. **Decision time:** This is when the rubber meets the road. You've compiled your REAL DEAL Wedding Budget. It's not going to be exact at this stage, but it's grounded in reality. It's the closest indicator you can have of what your wedding is actually going to cost. Compare this number with the number you and your Bankrollers have discussed. It's time to get real: Can you afford the wedding you want, or do you need to make adjustments?

   For some, this is a huge wake-up call. What you thought would be your $25,000 wedding is revealed to be your $40,000 wedding. But believe us when we tell you: You've saved yourself a lot of heartache and stress by figuring this out early. You have to be realistic about what's possible. If your heart is set on having the seaside wedding that will cost more than you thought, you'll need to find more money elsewhere, persuade your Bankroller(s) to provide additional funds, or go with another venue. The good news is that you've done your research and can speak knowledgeably about what vendors cost and what it will take to finance your wedding.

Additional expenses to consider when creating your REAL DEAL Budget:

Wedding Attire: Most people will have a number in mind for how much they're willing to spend on their wedding gown. For instance, given that the average price of a wedding dress in the United States is around $1,800[9], you might budget $2,000, find a dress you love for $1,999 and think, "Great! I'm on budget!" Not so fast. Wedding dress alterations can cost hundreds of dollars. Most likely you'll also buy a headpiece, veil, shoes, jewelry, a bag, and special undergarments for the gown. Also, a popular trend gaining steam is a second, more casual reception dress. And last, don't forget the groom's attire, whether it's a rental tuxedo or a new suit and shoes. While this may be a category you're not going to get multiple price estimates for, make certain the number you put down in your budget under "wedding attire" covers all these potential expenses.

Rentals: Some couples may want a level of design that can only be obtained through a rental company that offers many design elements like linens, chairs, and table décor to name a few. We didn't put them in our Top 10 Categories of Wedding Vendors list because we suggest holding off on researching this category until you have a better sense of the rest of your budget and what services the venue offers. Many venues offer upgrades to linens and chairs, which may be enough for you. Find out what your venue offers before making a decision about additional rentals.

Ceremony Venue: If you're going to get married in the same location as your reception, there may be an additional fee to factor in for the ceremony. If you plan to get married in a separate place of worship, this is typically a place you've already chosen, which is why we didn't include it in the Top 10. But that cost also needs to be included in your REAL DEAL Wedding Budget.

----

[9] Kim Forrest, "More Couples Than You Think Go Over Their Wedding Budget (and Here's How Much They Overspend)," March 3, 2022, https://www.theknot.com/content/how-many-couples-spend-over-budget

Officiant: The charge for someone to conduct your ceremony could be anywhere from $200 to more than $1,000, depending on whether it's a justice of the peace, a clergy member, or another type of celebrant.

Transportation: You may want transportation (like a limo) to drive the wedding party and VIPs to the ceremony and reception. For a destination wedding or if you have guests staying at a hotel, you might provide transportation to the venue if it's off-site. If it fits within your budget, offering transportation for your guests is a generous gesture. While transportation is an important consideration, it may be too early in your planning to know your exact needs. We suggest putting a placeholder in your budget for this expense.

Parking: If you're getting married in a venue where parking can be pricey (such as a downtown hotel), you might consider covering this cost for your guests. Venue managers or wedding planners can help you arrange validation of parking tickets and other logistics. Again, if you can afford it, it's a lovely gesture.

Lighting: Lighting effects can add a lot to your event visually by making your centerpieces pop, creating ambiance, and enhancing your personal brand. Businesses that offer these services can range from specialized lighting companies to your DJ/band, depending on the complexity of your needs. If this is what you want, we suggest you get some quotes. It can add thousands of dollars to your budget.

Insurance: When it comes to wedding insurance, there are generally two types available: liability and cancellation. Liability typically covers bodily injury and property damage. Most venues and vendors will have liability insurance, but we suggest you check, especially if your event takes place in a nontraditional space. Cancellation insurance tends to cover costs associated with cancelling the event due to circumstances beyond control, such as illness and weather. This may also recover payments for vendors if they are unable to complete their obligations due to unforeseeable circumstances. Policies can range from a few hundred dollars on up, depending on your coverage needs.

Tips: Just as you tip your restaurant server and your Uber driver, you'll want to tip the people that work your wedding and do an amazing job. You won't need to add a tip if gratuity is included in the contract, so be sure to find out. Vendors will appreciate the acknowledgment of a job well done.

Taxes and Fees: When you're gathering pricing, make sure you understand whether the prices quoted include any taxes, fees, or surcharges. These additional fees can add up.

Miscellaneous Items: There will be a number of smaller items you may want to have. These could include favors for your guests, gifts for your wedding party, goodie bags at the hotel for out-of-town guests, welcome signs, guest books, or toiletry basket in the restrooms. Just look on Etsy and you'll find countless accessories for a wedding day. While these items are not a lot of money individually, they will add up as a whole.

If you simply can't afford the number determined in your REAL DEAL Wedding Budget, then you need to make some tough decisions and adjust accordingly.

THE BIGGEST FACTORS THAT INFLUENCE YOUR BUDGET

The biggest budget influencers are **guest list, venue, date/timing,** and **priorities.** It's important to think about these factors early in your planning to help you stay within your budget.

Guest List: How many people will be at your wedding? When it comes to the wedding budget, the size of the guest list is important. The difference in cost between 100 and 200 guests is substantial. A bigger guest list means you're purchasing more food, more table centerpieces, and so on. Your budget will go further and allow for more customization with a smaller guest list. (We will cover more on this in chapter 5.)

Venue: What you spend on the venue (assuming it includes food and beverage) should be approximately 50% of your total budget. Remember, if your budget is $30,000, you can't spend $25,000 on your venue because you'll only have $5,000 left to pay at least nine other vendors. Just as you wouldn't want to buy a house that's over your budget, leaving no money for furniture, you don't want to put all your money into a venue with little left for flowers, photography, entertainment, and more. We explain food and beverage costs and why they're so important for your decision-making process in extensive detail in chapter 5. Start smart from a foundation you can afford so there's money available for all the special touches to make your wedding fabulous and personal.

Are you looking to have a destination wedding or stay local? Do you envision a city-chic vibe or a laid-back wedding in the countryside? The location dictates style, cost, and overall experience. The venue may be reasonably priced, but if the location requires travel and hotel expenses, will it be cost-prohibitive for family and friends to attend? Another important thing to keep in mind is the proximity of the venue to you, your family, and your vendors. Being far from the venue will necessitate more travel (and time off from work). Many vendors will ask for reimbursement of travel costs if they need to travel an hour or more. These are all factors you must consider before deciding on a venue. Are there better options that meet your general criteria and vision? Should you rethink your vision? These are the types of questions you need to ask yourself. Maybe that downtown ballroom with the city views you love so much is going to max out your budget, but the golf club on the hill a few miles away has a similar view. What are you really paying for—the room, the location, the reputation—and is it crucial to your vision?

Date/Timing: Most weddings happen on Saturday evening in the months that have predictably nice weather. That is usually the most convenient time for you and your guests, but those dates come at a premium for venues. Take a moment to consider having your wedding in an off-peak season, on a different day of the week, or time of day. These are ways to potentially reduce costs. Some venues offer incentives for booking in the off-season. There may also be more options for added values, such as a complimentary late-night snack, extended hour at the end of the night, or extra hotel rewards points. If you or your guests are traveling to the destination, hotel and airfare may cost more at peak seasons. People tend to eat and drink less during daytime affairs. If you consider a brunch or luncheon reception, you'll reduce your costs. Keep in mind, though, there's a reason these options are sometimes not appealing. Weather might be unpredictable, Sunday evenings are not as convenient for guests, and nighttime affairs can have a more party-like atmosphere.

Lastly, you could consider extending the length of your engagement. This option will give you more time to save up for your "must-haves."

Priorities: Hit the pause button and ask yourself what's most important to you for your wedding. Yes, it can be tough to discover that what you want doesn't align with your financial reality, but you can still achieve your essential vision by focusing on your priorities and must-haves. Continue to refer back to the vision statement you created in chapter 3.

MANAGING YOUR PRIORITIES

Managing your priorities is a balancing act—one you need to think about continually throughout your journey. Regardless of how well you plan, your priorities will evolve as the process unfolds and new situations arise. It happens to everyone. Here are a few tips on how to proactively manage your priorities:

Keep an open dialogue: Check in regularly with your committee (Bankroller and VIPs) to share key developments.

Revisit and reconsider: Are you on track or should you reconsider your priorities based on new circumstances? This is especially important after your budget has been created. Perhaps knowing the cost difference between a 10-piece band and a DJ will make you reconsider how important live music is to you.

Cross-check against your budget: Are you staying within your budget or do you need to make any adjustments? You've padded your budget to account for the unexpected, but that doesn't mean spending can go unchecked.

Keep everything in perspective: Every decision can seem like a top priority. That's why it's a good idea to take a step back and look at the big picture. Ultimately, this day is about marrying the person you love and being with friends and family. At the end of your wedding day, you and your partner are married and that is all that matters. Keeping things in perspective can go a long way toward minimizing the stress and indecisiveness that accompany changing priorities.

Remember, when you take the time to create your REAL DEAL Wedding Budget and consider each item within your underlying vision, you'll have smarter, more productive interactions with your partner, Bankroller(s), VIPs, and vendors. That's a win-win for everyone.

AN ALTERNATIVE TO BUILDING YOUR OWN BUDGET

If you absolutely hate all this budget stuff, you can hire a wedding planner who can help alleviate some of the mystery of this process. A good wedding planner will help you create and stick to a budget that aligns with your vision. They have established industry relationships, will guide you on vendor selection, negotiate on your behalf, and create the wedding you envisioned at the best possible price point. Of course, you'll need to find a planner that's right for you, but it can be well worth the effort, saving you time, your sanity, and even money. People often think they can't afford a planner, but that's not necessarily the case. In chapter 6, we discuss the advantages of using a wedding planner with some tips on how to find a good one.

REAL DEAL LIFE EXAMPLE #5:

Alex & Drew

Alex and Drew found the ideal setting for their mountainside wedding. Located in New Hampshire, the venue was a boutique-style resort and spa, offering stunning views of the White Mountains. It was the perfect location that showcased everything they loved about living in New Hampshire. They received an initial quote of $42,000 for food and beverage for 150 people and the use of the resort for the ceremony and reception. With a budget of $50,000, they knew it would be tight, but they were IN LOVE. They booked it, leaving them $8,000 for flowers, music, photographer, videographer, attire, wedding cake, and invitations.

Can you guess what happened? Yep, they went way over budget.

If Rachel's story sounds familiar, it's because it's one of the most common mistakes we see. Overspending on your venue sets off a domino effect of more ill-advised decisions. "Venue poor" couples become stressed out, spending more than they intended or cutting costs in other areas.

Those who put all their eggs in the venue basket inevitably end up cutting back in other critical areas. This approach only emphasizes what's lacking. You want your guests to be comfortable and enjoy themselves. You're much better off going with an affordable venue and adding fun and creative touches to create an amazing experience your guests will remember for the *right* reasons.

REAL DEAL LIFE EXAMPLE #6:

Sarah

Sarah was organized and feeling in control. She collected the most amazing images to help her create a romantic winter ceremony and reception. Using a wedding calculator and doing online research, she determined what she should pay for each vendor and allocated her money accordingly.

However, once she started gathering quotes, she went into sticker shock. Her vendors gave her quotes hundreds, if not thousands, more than her research indicated it would cost. Were her vendors overcharging or was her research flawed?

The answer is neither. Wedding calculators, cost averages, and other reports have become popular tools for wedding planning. They provide estimates based on general averages or defined sets of criteria. They're most accurate when choices are limited to a menu of predetermined options (such as with all-inclusive wedding packages). For the most part, when you use these tools, you're getting a price quote for a prepackaged experience based on the most popular preferences and what the local market will bear. As such, use these tools as a starting point only, otherwise they can be painfully misleading.

The beautiful images Sarah collected—gorgeous centerpieces, chandelier lights, floral canopies—were not average. So, if you're looking to create a personalized wedding experience, online wedding quotes won't be accurate for you. It's like getting the base price of a car: after you add extras such as upgraded stereo, leather, and sport mode, the price rises significantly. Multiply that scenario across 10 or more vendors, and your costs skyrocket.

Building a budget is the most stressful part of wedding planning. Couples find inspiration everywhere and are able to source ideas from around the globe.

The three biggest megatrends affecting wedding costs are:

1. Weddings are no longer a singular event but "an experience".

2. The internet offers endless options and choices.

3. Couples expect greater personalization.

**Use Our Five-Step Method to Build Your
REAL DEAL Wedding Budget:**

1. Look at the big picture and don't worry about wedding timetables until you've completed the planning process.

2. Find your Top 10 vendors using Google searches, visiting websites and getting recommendations from people you know.

3. Contact each vendor using our REAL DEAL email script.

4. Add up your estimates, then pad that number by 20%, at a minimum (and consider padding by 30 to 40% if you can).

5. Decision time. Can you afford your REAL DEAL Wedding Budget, or is it time to adjust your vision?

The biggest budget influencers and how to decrease costs:

1. **Guest List:** Cutting your guest list can save money. The more people that attend, the more you'll spend on items such as food and flowers.

2. **Venue:** Your venue should be approximately 50 percent of your budget. Don't be venue poor. It's better to book a less expensive venue so there's enough money left for your remaining vendors.

3. **Date/Timing:** Is it worth it to change to an off-peak date, time, or day of the week to save money? Are there incentives that the venue may offer you for an off-peak booking?

4. **Priorities:** Compare your REAL DEAL Wedding Budget with your wedding vision. Decide on your "must-haves" and "non-negotiables" and put your money toward those areas first. Get creative and flexible with lower-priority items.

5. **Other budget influencers:** Can you find a venue closer to home or work with vendors closer to the venue to avoid travel surcharges? Does it make sense to have a longer engagement period to save additional money?

Alternatively, consider hiring a wedding planner to bypass this entire process. They can help plan your budget, select your vendors, and negotiate the best terms on your behalf.

CHAPTER
5

---- ◆ ----

BUILDING YOUR GUEST LIST
& CHOOSING YOUR

You've established your REAL DEAL budget, had frank financial discussions with your Bankroller(s), and established your vision for your ideal wedding. Now that you're done with the preplanning research and have laid the groundwork, you're fully ready to hit the ground running on your wedding planning!

The Guest List

WHY YOUR GUEST LIST SHOULD COME FIRST

Deciding the number of people you will have at your wedding is a very important step to take before you make any other decisions. It will affect the size of the venue you choose as well as your budget. So, yes, figuring out which of your colleagues or whether great-aunt Claire makes the cut is hugely important!

While it may seem counterintuitive, it's actually correct to build your guest list before you decide on a venue. You don't want to fall in love with a venue only to discover that you have more people to invite than it will hold. It's far easier to find a venue that will fit your list than to cut your list to fit a venue.

Keep in mind that the size of the wedding is one of the biggest budget influencers (see chapter 4). Many items you're purchasing are priced per person. So, the larger the guest list, the more money you're spending in total. See page 81 for a table that lists which vendors charge by the person and which typically don't.

HOW TO BUILD YOUR GUEST LIST

A wedding guest list is incredibly nuanced and personal. This isn't just any party—it's a life milestone. While you may not have spoken to your best friend from elementary school in decades, all of a sudden you may find yourself remembering the pact you made while on the playground and wonder if you should invite her. This is up to you, of course.

VENDOR TYPE	PER PERSON	PER JOB
Venue Rental		✓
Caterer (Food/Beverage)	✓	
Entertainment		✓
Photography		✓
Videography		✓
Flowers	✓ (More guests = more tables = more centerpieces. More bridesmaids = more bouquets, etc.)	
Invitations	✓ (per person/couple/family)	
Cake	✓	
Favors	✓	
Rentals	✓	
Lighting		✓
Transportation	✓ (possibly, the more people in the wedding party or more guests means more vehicles needed)	
Beauty (Hair/Makeup)	✓	
Ceremony (Venue/Officiant)		✓

Here are some practical steps to build a comprehensive guest list:

- First things first. The Bankrollers and VIPs have a say in who and how many people get invites. You may not have a personal connection with your dad's boss, but he does, and if he's footing the bill, it's important to give his needs consideration. Similarly, VIPs should also be given the opportunity to add to the list. For example, if parents aren't financially contributing, they may still want to invite a few friends—let them. It's their celebration, too, and they may want to share their joy.

- Have Bankrollers and VIPs (this includes you, the couple!) independently make two lists of people to invite: the Wish List and the Must List. The Wish List is all those who they hope can come. The Must List is not up for negotiation—there might as well not be a wedding if these folks can't make it.

- Next, put the Wish Lists and Must Lists together and count them up to see the difference in size. If your combined lists add to a manageable number, then great! You're ready to look for venues that can accommodate that group. If the number is much larger than you were thinking, start with the Must Lists as a baseline, and see how many people from the Wish List you can add before it starts to get too big.

- If your guest list is still too large, consider making a B List. This is a list of people that will only be invited after you have confirmation that people on your A List will not attend your wedding. If you plan to do this, give yourself enough time to mail a second round of invitations to your B List, so you will receive their RSVPs with enough time to plan for your final guest count.

Practical Things to Consider:

Children: Do you want your wedding to be kid-friendly? How many young children are in the family? How important is it for them to be at the wedding? Will the parents have more or less fun if the kids are there? Do they need babysitters?

Family: How deep into the family tree will you go? Will you have your cousin whom you haven't seen in years? Will you invite all your second cousins because you're close with one and feel the need to be fair? How important is it to "do the right thing" in the eyes of your extended family? This is tough. You have to weigh what's right for you versus what is expected versus what you can afford.

Plus-Ones: Can everyone bring a date or just people who are married/in a long-term relationship? What constitutes a long-term relationship?

Try to have these conversations with an open mind and with as little emotion as possible. One thing to remember: choose a venue that will accommodate your whole guest list. Assume everyone will come. Of course, there will be attrition and most of the time it's in the range of 10 to 20%. But you can't anticipate what that final guest count will be prior to the RSVPs. You'd be surprised at the efforts guest will make to attend a wedding. Hoping that guests don't come so you'll fit in your venue is stressful!

The Wedding Venue

After deciding whether to use a wedding planner (more about this in chapter 6), choosing your venue should be your next big decision. It plays a crucial role in your overall experience. From the day you sign that contract through the entire planning process, you'll be working closely with your venue.

As much as you may want to get things moving, don't rush this step. You need time to properly vet your options. Schedule meetings and tour every venue you're seriously considering. It's best to experience the venue firsthand to determine whether the space fits your vision.

HERE'S A LIST OF FACTORS TO KEEP IN MIND WHEN CHOOSING A VENUE:

Venue type: Venues typically fall into three general categories:

- **Traditional:** hotels, catering halls, country clubs
- **Unique:** historic homes, lofts, barns, gardens, museums
- **Alternative:** ski slopes, public parks, bowling alleys, your backyard

Consider the pros and cons of each type of venue. To get started, use our "Venue Categories and Questions to Ask" chart (page 87). The venue will have a major impact on your time, money, and stress level. It's crucial to consider every angle. Venues that seem "easy," such as your parents' backyard, can end up being more complicated and costlier than imagined because everything from the dance floor to portable restrooms to catering has to be brought in or built.

We don't have a strong preference for venue type. We've planned beautiful weddings at industrial lofts, a car museum, an aquarium, and a converted firehouse. Like the idea of a zoo? Think about how a howler monkey might sound during the ceremony. Does the firehouse sound fun? You should know that your guests may be tempted to slide down the pole. We've seen it! We love all types of weddings, including the unusual ones. But we want you to go in with your eyes wide open, with a full understanding of what's involved.

Questions: You need to not only determine whether the venue is within your price range, but also whether it will work from a practical standpoint. What type of support will you receive from the staff? Is the layout logical, with easy access to the bathrooms and bar? Is the venue handicapped-accessible? Is the reception area one large, open space or is it broken up into smaller rooms? Will it comfortably accommodate the number of guests you're planning on having? Does the advertised seating capacity of 200 really mean 160 when you add a dance floor? Is there temperature control (AC/heat)? Are there time constraints? Are there sound constraints (city ordinance)? These are all crucial points to consider when selecting a venue.

Your guest list: The experience and comfort of your guests should be a top priority. The venue should suit your guests as well as you. No one wants friends and family grumbling about the logistics before the festivities even begin. Ever complain about having to drive in rush-hour traffic to get to a six o'clock wedding on a Friday night? Ask yourself, "Will it be difficult, impractical, or cost-prohibitive for my guests to attend this wedding?" You can't please everyone, but if your desired venue is burdensome for a significant portion of your guests, then maybe it's not the best choice. Look for ways your guests can be accommodated. Can you arrange group transportation or discounted hotel rates? Consider every aspect of the guest experience before signing that contract.

Your emotions: Keeping your emotions in check is a biggie. We've seen the most levelheaded people get swept away by the beauty of a mountain vista or the elegance of a ballroom with twinkling chandeliers, only to disregard potential drawbacks. You might really connect with the venue manager and want to work with her, but if the space isn't quite right, don't sign the contract. Ten months down the road, that venue manager may no longer be working at the venue. Remember you're hiring the venue and not the venue manager. The point is, yes, it needs to "feel right," but you also need to be conscious about whether the space is going to work for your wedding. A mistake we see often is a couple trying to squeeze the wedding into a venue that's too small. They'll say, "It's gorgeous. I

Being unrealistic about the venue and your needs is just asking for headaches down the road.

know the space maxes out at 150 and we have 180 people on our guest list, but we're sure the out-of-town relatives won't come." Famous last words.

Documentation: When visiting venues (or talking to any vendor, for that matter) there are a lot of details to remember. You'll be excited by what you see, imagining your own wedding, and you'll be so distracted that you won't absorb the details of your visit. Write notes, use voice memo, and snap photos to recall key pieces of information and your general impressions.

Your Wedding Committee: Once you've narrowed down your venue options, talk with your Bankroller and relevant VIPs to review your choices. The venue (combined with food and beverage) is the biggest financial investment in your wedding. You need to make sure everyone who matters is on board before you sign that contract. You want agreement among the important players. If you've followed our steps, then you've already thought through their key concerns and will be prepared to make a convincing case for the venue of your choice.

Venue Categories And Questions To Ask

Traditional Spaces	Unique Spaces	Alternative Spaces
• Hotels • Function halls • Country clubs	• Historic sites, including houses, farms, barns, mansions, gardens • Museums • Libraries • Zoos or aquariums • Restaurants • Professional athletic stadiums	• Someone's home • Bowling alleys, ice rinks, rock climbing gyms, and other entertainment venues • Outdoor locations with scenic vistas, such as beaches, parks, etc.

SERVICE EXPECTATION

We'll take care of you. Weddings are our business.	*We like to host weddings, but they're not our main priority or focus.*	*You can use our space, but you're on your own.*
• Dedicated event manager • Familiar with running weddings • Big part of their business • Have dedicated staff and support team for day of • Usually offer specialty wedding packages and upgrades • Have all the necessary equipment on-site (linens, chairs, etc.) • Have on-site catering • Hotels will have rooms and wedding suite options for both guests and the couple • On-site ceremony space • On-site space for getting ready	• Site manager may or may not have experience coordinating weddings at their location • Host weddings with varying levels of expertise, resources, and support • Weddings are often a supplementary source of income • There may be unique restrictions placed on the wedding (time it can be held, materials allowed on-site, food restrictions, etc.) • May or may not have necessary equipment on-site (chairs, linens) • May or may not have on-site catering	• No on-site support or expertise, just a point of contact to coordinate the agreement or contract with (sometimes) • Everything will have to be brought in, from the catering to the portable restrooms • Everything will be managed by you and the people you hire or bring in to help

QUESTIONS TO ASK

Traditional Spaces

- Will I have an assigned event manager to work with me? If yes . . .
  - *How involved or available will they be throughout planning process?*
  - *How long have they been working in the industry? (to get a sense of their level of expertise)*
  - *Will they be with me on the day of and for how long?*

- What type of support will I have day of?

- What does your price include? (food/beverage, venue space, etc.)

- Is there a food/beverage minimum? (and will your expected number of guests meet that minimum?)

- What is the maximum number of people your space can fit? (and what is the recommended number for comfortable seating?)

- Are there additional fees I can expect? Examples include:
  - *Service room fee*
  - *Site fees*
  - *Chairs, linens, and other upgrades*
  - *Extended hours*
  - *Ceremony fee*
  - *Gratuities, taxes, administration fees*
  - *Bridal suite rental*
  - *Parking/valet, coat-check fees*
  - *Cake-cutting fee*
  - *Bar service and waitstaff fees*

- Does your venue have restrictions? (time constraints, food, materials that can be brought in)

- Can your venue accommodate any of my restrictions or unique circumstances, including food requirements, allergies, accessibility, etc.?

- How many weddings do you do a year? (The more weddings a venue does, the more experience and on-site expertise they will likely have)

- How many weddings do you do in a single day? If you do more than one in a single day, are they at the same time? And will I ever cross paths with the other wedding party?

- Can I bring in outside food or beverage for any part of the wedding?

- Are there certain vendors that I am required to work with? (important to know if you want to bring in your own favorite vendor)

QUESTIONS TO ASK

Unique Spaces

Ask all the questions listed under Traditional, PLUS . . .

- Does the cost of the space include catering?

- Who provides the catering?

- If the venue doesn't provide catering, do I have to find someone on my own or do you have a preferred list?

- Is there temperature control in the space?

Alternative Spaces

Ask all the questions listed under Traditional and Unique Spaces PLUS . . .

- What liability will I incur by hosting my wedding in this location?

- Will I need insurance?

- Do I need a permit, police detail, or special permissions?

UNDERSTANDING IN-HOUSE VERSUS OFF-PREMISE CATERING AND BEVERAGE COSTS

What you spend on your food and beverage costs combined with the venue rental will be the majority of your budget. How you purchase the food and drink you serve your guests will depend on the type of venue you choose. For example, a hotel or country club will likely have a full catering department in-house, while a historic home or a more nontraditional venue may require hiring an off-premise catering company to prepare the food on-site.

In-House Catering: If you choose a venue that provides the food in-house, they very often have minimums. Sometimes a venue will have a minimum for what you spend per person on food. This type of minimum may also require a guarantee of a minimum number of guests. Many venues will have a food and beverage minimum. This will be a large sum that a client would have to spend on food and beverage regardless of how many people attend the event. This minimum is usually higher on popular days (Saturdays) and times of year (June). Typically, if your guest count gets close to the maximum that can fit in the space, you will easily meet the minimum. But if you have fewer people, you may end up adding food (extra appetizers or an additional dinner course) to meet the minimum.

Understand that this amount has to be spent on food and beverage before tax and fees apply. The tax and fees do not contribute to your food and beverage minimum spend. When looking at venues and requesting proposals, ensure that you ask for all taxes and fees that apply so you can see the overall cost. Keep in mind that the administration fee can also be anywhere from 10 to 35%. Tax changes depending on the location (state, meal tax). Other venues may not have a minimum but charge a set rental fee apart from your per-guest cost. This fee can sometimes be negotiated or waived.

Off-Premise Catering: When you choose a venue that does not provide catering, you will need to hire an off-premise catering company to come into the venue and do everything from preparing the meals to serving and cleaning up. Many of these venues will have a list of caterers they recommend. The venue will charge a rental fee, which generally covers the use of the space and any chairs and tables they have available. The catering company will charge a per-person fee for food and then additional fees for equipment (plates, glasses, silverware, chaffing dishes etc.) It's important to understand, when comparing in-house versus off-premise catering services, that the per-person price for the food tends to cost more with in-house catering. However, these in-house prices include all of the equipment that the off-site caterers will list as a separate fee. Those rentals add up and can equal or surpass a traditional venue that includes food and beverage.

Beverage Costs: Many venues offer beverage packages along with their catering. Depending on their licenses, off-premise caterers will either include beverages in their services or coordinate with a beverage provider on your behalf. When considering beverage packages, think about your guests. Do you have a young crowd who you anticipate will drink heavily and celebrate from the start of the party? Or do you have a lot of older relatives attending who don't drink at all? Keep in mind that all beverages will contribute to the food and beverage minimum. If your budget allows, host the bar when possible. Venues and caterers offer a number of ways to control your bar costs:

Full Hosted Bar (Package): You pay a flat rate per-person for unlimited drinks for a set amount of time. This is a popular option if you know your guests will drink a lot of alcohol.

Full Hosted Bar (Consumption): You pay for the number of drinks consumed during the event. If you do select this option, you should be able to review the consumption sheet and bar tab at the end of the event before you are charged.

Partially Hosted Bar: Many venues offer catering packages that include one hour of a full hosted bar during the cocktail hour. Following the cocktail hour, the bar becomes cash, so guests are responsible for purchasing their own drinks. Some venues may also include one to two glasses of wine served with dinner.

Limited Bar: Some venues hold a license that only allows them to sell beer and wine. If you have an off-premise caterer and have the option to choose which beverages to serve, you could limit to beer, wine, soft drinks, and perhaps a signature cocktail. Some venues will give you options or tiers of liquor selections. In that case, there may be a base option with standard liquor (beer, wine, gin, vodka, whiskey) to which you can add more options, such as the top-shelf liquor or cordials.

Consumption Bar with a Cap: This option is when you offer a hosted bar with a maximum spend limit. As the bar tab approaches the bar cap, your venue manager will let you know, and they will discreetly change the bar over to a cash bar. If you're getting close to the wedding date (a couple of weeks out) and realize you have some money left in the budget, this could be a last-minute add-on.

Signature Cocktail: Many venues will allow you to select signature cocktails. This can either be displayed at the bar or passed to guests as they enter the cocktail hour. This can be a fun way to personalize the bar menu.

Summary

Some important things to remember when building a guest list:

- The size of the guest list will help determine the cost of the wedding and what type of venue you will have.
- Remember to consult with Bankrollers and VIPs when putting together the guest list.
- Put together a Must List and a Wish List of guests, then put those together with the same lists from your Bankrollers and VIPs, then build from there.
- Ask yourself:
  - Do you want kids at the wedding?
  - How deep into the family tree would you like to go?
  - Who will be allowed to bring a plus-one?

Picking the venue comes next:

- Decide the type of venue you want: traditional, unique, or alternative.
- Ask the right questions when vetting the space.
- Think about every aspect of your guests' experience.
- Document your impressions during venue visits by taking photographs and notes.
- Bring your Wedding Committee into the process for final approval.
- Understand your options for in-house versus off-premise catering.
- Consider various beverage options and costs.

CHAPTER

6

◆

ASSEMBLING YOUR

Vendor Team

When it comes to working with vendors, you don't know what you don't know. Unless you've planned a wedding before, you won't know which questions to ask or what will become important to you down the road.

At this point in your planning you've put important foundations in place. It may not seem like it, but you've accomplished so much!

- You've assembled your Wedding Committee, chosen your venue, discussed your priorities, and drafted a guest list.
- You've created your Wedding Vision Statement and portfolio to guide you forward.
- You've built your REAL DEAL budget, reflecting the true cost of your wedding.

Now it's time to hire your vendor team.

What A Wedding Planner Can Do For You

After months of planning and anticipation, your wedding day will come and go in a flash. How do you want to spend it? Running around managing the details or enjoying your guests and creating wonderful memories? Be honest with yourself. Are you an easygoing "go-with-the-flow" type who doesn't sweat the small stuff? Or are you a Type-A personality who needs place cards laid out just so? What makes you comfortable?

Our recommendation, of course, would be to hire a reputable wedding planner, but you may be asking yourself, "Is a planner really necessary? Why can't I do this stuff on my own?"

Our response: How many weddings have you planned before? Do you know how to make sure events go smoothly on the actual wedding day? Do you know that the average couple spends over 500 hours planning their wedding?[9] Do you know which public parks require permits in order to take photos? Do you know what a fair price is for the rentals you want and the options available to you? Do you even know what rentals *are*?

A wedding planner can help you navigate the tricky waters of wedding planning as well as provide a 360-degree view of the event to oversee what's happening and coordinate the who, what, when, and where of the big day.

Here's a good analogy: If you were building a house, you'd hire a general contractor to coordinate your subcontractors and make certain your house was built to plan. The general contractor takes care of the permits, contracts, and other details you never knew building a house entailed. Your wedding planner is like the general contractor for your event. They make sure every decision supports and enhances your vision.

It's often a misconception that planning a wedding is easy to do yourself. You may figure that, between you and your venue manager, you're all set. A venue manager cares about your wedding and the outcome. Many go above and beyond their job description. However, the venue manager works for the venue, while a wedding planner works solely for you. Your planner will be looking out for a million things that aren't your venue manager's responsibility but are vital to the success of your wedding.

Your venue manager will plan a timeline from the moment you enter their space until the end of the event. (For example, the timing for the first course, first dance, cake cutting, etc.) Your planner will troubleshoot the timeline for the whole day, making sure that if you have a 5:30 p.m. ceremony, there's enough time for hair, makeup, photos, getting to the church, oh, and eating at some point. A full-service planner does all of this for you. They're with you from the very beginning of the planning process to the end of the event.

....

[9] SWNS, "Engaged couples."

Because planning weddings is, quite literally, a wedding planner's job, they are familiar with not only the technical ins and outs of the process, but the major players in the industry. Wedding planners are vital members of the wedding community, building relationships and trust with various vendors for every wedding they plan. Those hard-won relationships can save you a lot of time, headaches, and money, making the money you spend on hiring a wedding planner a *very* good investment.

The earlier you can involve the planner in your wedding process, the more benefits you will receive. They make sure your day is seamless as if their job depends on it—because it does. Your planner is prepared to handle whatever is thrown at them throughout the process, from aspects as simple as invitation etiquette to the complex navigation of coordinating timelines with multiple vendors. They'll notice details you won't, and they'll know how to react quickly.

Planning a wedding is like producing a live show in many ways. Would you put on a play without a director? Would you defend yourself in court without a lawyer? There's a lot at stake when it comes to your wedding. Hiring a professional planner streamlines the process and alleviates your work and much of the stress. And that can completely transform your entire experience—making the planning something pleasant, as it should be!

TYPES OF WEDDING PLANNING SERVICES

Wedding planning services commonly fall into two categories: logistics and vision. Logistics covers vendor selection, budgeting, timelines, transportation, hotel blocks, and day-of management, just to name a few. Vision is the overall experience of your event. The planner gives input into floral design, lighting, rentals, invitations, branding, and everything else that affects the look and experience of your wedding.

Professional planners often offer a number of options:

Full Service: This is the whole shebang, from venue selection to packing up your family photo display at the end of the night. You hire this planner at the very beginning of the process.

Vendor Selection: This is what you need if you'd like guidance on finding the right vendors. A wedding planner can help you streamline the process. They know the vendors and who would be a good fit for your needs.

Day-Of Services: This is when a planner works with you for four to eight weeks prior to the wedding to make certain everything runs smoothly on the big day. (Chapter 7 goes into wedding day management in more detail.)

Customized Packages: Planners will custom design a package specifically for your needs.

If you choose not to hire a wedding planner, never fear: This chapter will help minimize the "don't knows" and help you make smart choices along the way.

Your Vendor Team

Now it's time to build the rest of your wedding team! If you've hired a planner, you're not doing this alone. If you haven't, you'll be vetting dozens of vendors providing a wide spectrum of services. Review your priorities. Does it make sense to DIY certain things? Can you save money by choosing a less-experienced professional over a more seasoned vendor in one of your low-priority areas? There's a lot to think about.

Some vendors will be easy to hire, others less so. We'd like to give you a magic formula, but there isn't one. Remember, your best friend might push a florist who is "perfect for you," but you need to click with that vendor.

COMPILING YOUR VENDOR LIST

The results of any initial broad online search will be overwhelming. There are more personal ways to find your vendors. As you go through this process, certain names will pop up again and again. Maybe your venue manager recommends a florist who was also recommended by your photographer. The names that keep bubbling up to the top of everyone's list are the vendors worth investigating further.

HOW TO FIND YOUR VENDORS

Family and Friends: A tried-and-true source and usually your first stop. Did you love the flowers at your friend's wedding last year? Definitely ask for the name of the florist. Your cousin's best friend is in a band you love? Maybe they would be willing to perform at your wedding. Tap into your network. When someone gives a recommendation, ask why they liked their vendor. The reasons will reveal if the same vendor would be a match for you. Remember to properly vet these vendors as you would any other vendor. What worked for your friend may not work for your style, vision, and budget.

Fact-Finding List: These are the 30+ vendors you initially reached out to as part of your fact-finding research from step two of our Five-Step Method to Build Your REAL DEAL Wedding Budget. This is a great list because a) you already did the work to find these vendors through wedding websites and other online searches, and b) you've received rough cost estimates.

Venue List: Most traditional and some unique-space venues maintain a list of preferred vendors. Ask your venue if they have such a list. Then find out how the list was compiled. Is it a list of their favorite vendors—the ones they trust and like working with? Or is it a list of vendors who paid to be included? Both types can be helpful in finding your team; just don't assume the list has been vetted by the venue.

Venue Manager's Favorites: If the venue manager has been working in the industry for a while, it's likely they will have favorites or opinions about certain vendors, including their level of professionalism or quality of work. This is important when it comes to ensuring a smooth wedding day. The manager's recommendations may or may not be on the venue list, so be sure to ask them.

Your Wedding Vendors: Wedding vendors know each other and have opinions on who's good based on their own experiences. Maybe the photographer you just hired has great things to say about a certain DJ or advice about an invitations vendor to use. By asking around, you'll get a feel for which vendors are respected within the community. Valuable insider knowledge is worth its weight in gold—and it's free!

Professional Organizations: There are many national organizations, such as NACE (National Association for Catering & Events), ILEA (International Live Event Association), and ABC (Association of Bridal Consultants) that have vendor listings on their websites. Additionally, there may be a local organization in your area. In Boston, we are proud members of the Boston Wedding Group.

After you secure the venue, reserving these vendors should be next on your list:

- Caterer (if your venue doesn't provide food and beverage)
- Entertainment (band, DJ, ceremony musicians)
- Photographer and/or videographer
- Florist
- Wedding dress

These services and items will be some of your biggest expenses after the venue and usually need to be booked far in advance. Start with your highest priorities, then work your way down your list. Lock these vendors in, sign contracts, and buy your dress. Once you've hired the vendor(s), planning the details can often wait, as most vendors will give you their own timetable for next steps.

Everyone Else

Your list of other vendors and additional items you'll purchase will also likely include some of the following:

- Invitations and other paper goods such as seating cards, menus, table numbers, thank-you cards
- Hair and makeup stylists
- Wedding officiant
- Specialized lighting
- Rentals for additional furniture (lounge areas, upgraded tables and chairs)
- Transportation for the wedding party and out-of-town guests
- Wedding cake and/or other dessert (donuts, pastries, etc.)
- Guest favors
- Photo booth or other fun additional activities
- Rehearsal dinner venue
- Day-after wedding brunch venue
- Welcome bags for out-of-town guests
- Gifts for the wedding party
- Fun signage (Example: "Welcome!" or "Mr. & Mrs.")

Keep working on your list. Don't wait until a month before your wedding to start thinking about finding a bakery for your cake. The best wedding planners pick their team early because it gives them plenty of time to think about overall design, plan logistics, and deal with unexpected issues. The one thing you can count on in planning your wedding is unexpected issues! Planning a wedding is stressful enough without rushing around two days before looking for last-minute items. Give yourself the luxury of time—believe us, it will be less stressful and more enjoyable for everyone involved.

Vetting Your Vendors

When you first reach out to vendors, they're going to need some basic information, including your date, venue, and the number of guests. All of this is easy enough to provide. But they also need to know your general budget to be sure it aligns with their pricing structure.

Here are a couple of things you can expect to share with your vendors:

Your budget: You've done your initial research and know the going rates in your area. You've thought through your priorities and set a budget that should be workable. This means you're in a good position to discuss your wedding and negotiate the best services.

Your inspiration photos you've collected: In addition to describing what you want, show it. Share images that showcase your vision, as well

REAL DEAL

FACT
12

If you want the best from your team, it's important to be open and honest. This isn't the time to be coy about your budget or what you want. Finding the right vendor means having an open two-way dialogue.

Picking a vendor shouldn't be solely about what they can do for you at what price—you also need to work well with each other. Is there good rapport? Does the vendor seem excited to be involved in your wedding?

as things you don't like. We're not just talking about images pertaining to that particular vendor, but every aspect of your wedding. If you're meeting with the florist, show them examples of flowers you like, but also bring images you've collected of the cake, décor, and the dress as well. Pictures are worth a thousand words—they give the vendor a more comprehensive sense of your style and vision.

It's possible that what you want will cost more than what you've allotted in your budget, but at least you can have a productive conversation about what's realistic once you've shared your budget. A helpful vendor will make suggestions for how to achieve your vision within your means. Listen and be open to their recommendations. Experienced vendors know how to create the biggest impact for what you're spending. You may have to make some compromises, but they can help you figure out what's most important and how to achieve it. If a vendor is truly outside of your price point, ask them for recommendations of vendors that can work with your budget.

You don't need to be best friends with every vendor, but you want to be able to work with them on a personal level. This is especially true for vendors who will be interacting with you on the wedding day, such as your photographer, DJ, or caterer. Think about how the vendor responds to your initial inquiry. Are they friendly? All business? Unprofessional? Does their style match yours? When communicating with them, do you feel heard or rushed off the phone? Trust your gut. Money is important, but you'll reap the biggest savings in time and your sanity if you focus on finding the best match rather than the lowest price.

Over the years, we've seen less reliance on face-to-face meetings with clients. Often all the interaction with a vendor can be accomplished via email, texts, and phone calls. Sometimes it's still helpful to have an in-person (or video) meeting. This is especially true for vendors that will have big hand in the overall look, feel, and experience of your wedding day, such as caterers and florists. That said, if you feel the need for a face-to-face meeting with a vendor, we don't recommend that until you've had an initial "feeling each other out" conversation. Otherwise it's a waste of your time and theirs. By the time you meet in person, you should be confident that this is your vendor. The in-person meeting should be the final step of your vetting process.

TIPS FOR VETTING YOUR VENDORS

When selecting potential vendors, you may click and feel like the person totally gets you. Fantastic! But that's not enough. You need to ask yourself, "Does this person have the right expertise? Do they run an ethical business? Do they have professional follow-through?" In short, you need to do your due diligence. You can uncover most of this information through basic online research and conversations with the vendor. Just be sure to get answers to the following questions:

What do other clients say? If you haven't done this already, take the time to go online and read reviews. But remember to keep it in perspective: One or two negative comments may not be a deal breaker, but if they have over 10 to 15% one- to two-star reviews, that would be a red flag. Pay special attention to three-star reviews as these may give you a different perspective and insight on that vendor.

Are they an established business? How long has the vendor been in business? Are they an experienced professional or just starting out? Having a nice website doesn't mean someone is experienced—it just means they're savvy about marketing. That definitely counts for something, but you still need to know whom you're hiring. You don't want someone who's all surface gloss with little substance underneath. (See our section **Weighing the Trade-Offs: Seasoned Professional vs. Newbie Professional vs. DIY** on page 110 for a more detailed discussion of the pros and cons of going with an established business versus a newbie.)

Do they belong to any professional wedding, catering, or trade organizations? Is the vendor networked into their community? If someone is committed to being a professional, they'll likely belong to wedding and trade organizations on both a national and local level. Of course, this doesn't tell you if they're right for you, but it gives you a sense of their commitment to their profession. Wedding planning is a collaborative industry, so people who are involved in trade organizations not only keep up with the latest trends but also know how to collaborate—a necessity when planning an event. Trade organizations may vary by region, but three of the biggest national wedding associations are NACE (National Association for Catering and Events), ILEA (International Live Events Association), and ABC (Association of Bridal Consultants). Look for local organizations that vet their members like the Boston Wedding Group (which we highly recommend as long-term members).

Do they specialize in weddings? Someone may be amazing at their craft, but if they haven't done many (or any) weddings, it should give you pause. There are things you need to know as a photographer, band, florist, and even hair stylist that are specific to weddings—logistics, timing, expectations. Of course, a less-experienced vendor may do a fantastic job, but it's important to know whether they have specialized experience so you can make an informed decision and align your expectations accordingly.

How many weddings or events do they do per year, per month, per weekend? How busy are they? It's great to have an in-demand vendor with lots of clients, but make certain your vendor has the capacity to support your event. If there are multiple events on the weekend of your wedding, how will that affect you? Ask the question and then decide how comfortable you are with the answers. You'll gain great insight into how their business is run.

Who will be my point person? Often a couple will meet with the owner of a business and think they've found the perfect fit. But once they sign the contract, they find themselves working with a junior associate, not the person they thought they hired. Make sure you understand the vendor's working process. How do they typically engage with clients and who will be your primary contact? Make sure you're happy with your point person before signing the contact.

Bottom line? *Trust your gut.* You need to feel good about your vendors and there should be chemistry. This is especially important for those vendors you'll be spending a lot of your day with, such as the photographer, DJ/band, venue manager, and your wedding planner. Even if your interactions are limited, you still want to feel like this person is on your team. These vendors are being invited into one of the most important and exciting events of your life! Their role is to help you, not add stress. Even if a vendor was perfect for your cousin, eliminate them from your list if you're not feeling a connection.

RED FLAGS
As with any industry, there are red flags to be mindful of.

Nonresponsiveness: We don't care how amazing a vendor's reputation is. If you have to chase them down, you're not going to be happy with the results. If you don't hear back from a vendor within one to two days during the workweek (unless they have an out-of-office reply), that's a red flag. You shouldn't expect instantaneous responses, but the vendor should reply quickly to acknowledge your inquiry at a minimum, and either answer your questions or let you know when they'll be available to do so. How a vendor responds to your initial inquiry is an indication of how responsive they'll be throughout the planning process.

Lack of connection: Someone may be great at their craft, but you may not feel an excitement or connection with them. Great wedding vendors genuinely love what they do and share in the excitement. If you're not feeling a genuine interest in your wedding from them, trust your gut—it's probably not there.

Sloppy and slapdash behavior: How someone presents themself to you in the beginning is what you can expect throughout the process. In other words, if the vendor is careless or forgetful in their communications, if their communications contain multiple errors, if they're not detail-oriented, if you have to keep reminding them of things—this is who the vendor is. They're not likely to change. If you're a Type-A personality, this may not work for you. Alternatively, perhaps you're willing to put up with some less-than-desirable behavior if it means getting a great artist on your team. You know yourself better than anyone, so make the decision you feel most comfortable with.

Getting The Most Out Of Your Vendors

Here are some tips to keep in mind when working with vendors.

Be open-minded: Share your ideas and be flexible and open to theirs. They may have a different approach or a unique method you haven't considered for how to express your vision. You've hired a professional because they are experts at what they do. When you trust your vendors, they'll be more excited and freer to expand their creativity, and ultimately, you'll get more from the experience.

Be honest: A well-meaning friend might suggest telling the vendor you're just having a big party or family reunion. We don't recommend that. It is true that some vendors charge more for weddings than other types of events, and maybe you're wondering why. Weddings are inherently more labor-intensive. Unlike a corporate event or party, there are more details to coordinate, more consultations and phone calls to arrange, and more negotiations to get things just right. More emotions and importance are attached to each decision, so the stakes are higher. You want your wedding to be perfect and so does your vendor. That means they will spend more time than they would on another kind of event, and they should be compensated for that time.

It's OK to ask: Some vendors are willing to negotiate. It comes down to the ask. Many vendors will be willing to make suggestions to help you, especially if you've made a personal connection. They often have ideas on how to accommodate your budget by suggesting ways to modify your vision yet achieve similar results.

Be patient: Vendors should be responsive. If not, you have a problem on your hands (see the previous section, Red Flags). We live in a 24/7 world, but there are limits. If you contact your vendor over the weekend, don't be surprised if you don't hear back until Monday. They could be working another wedding. Being respectful of each other's time always benefits both parties in collaboration.

Weighing The Trade-Offs: Seasoned Professional vs. Newbie Professional vs. Do-It-Yourself (DIY)

Unless money is no object (and seriously, how many people have that luxury?), you're going to have to weigh your time, money, and priorities, and make decisions accordingly. Should you hire the renowned high-end photographer, or will the young professional just starting their own studio be a great alternative? Do you need to charter a coach bus to shuttle your guests or would Uber or Lyft be just fine? Maybe you'd like to bake your own wedding cake or design your invitations online. Don't assume DIY is always the way to go. What you save in money, you may lose in time and gain in stress. If you decide to DIY certain aspects of your wedding, we highly recommend not taking on anything that requires last-minute preparation. There are better things to do in the 24 hours before walking down the aisle than making 200 fondant rose petals. However, hiring an experienced professional for every single detail may not be the right option either. Perhaps you'll use a mix of DIY, seasoned professionals, and newbie professionals. Use the following chart to understand the pros and cons of each to help decide what's right for you.

THE PROS AND CONS OF THE SEASONED PRO, NEWBIE PRO, AND DIY

SEASONED PRO
Experienced in their craft and the wedding industry

Why You Hire Them	What to Be Aware Of
• They have proven experience with references.	• You'll be paying more for the expertise.
• They know what they're doing and are prepared to deal with every situation or problem that comes up.	• Depending on the size of the vendor, you may not be dealing with the founder, but rather with someone more junior.
• They've seen what works and what doesn't, and can provide valuable guidance.	• Being in the industry for a long time can sometimes lead to being stuck in a certain routine or not wanting to deal with new ideas because they've "been there, done that".
• They are business savvy and tend to have implemented processes that make it easy to work with them.	
• They have industry connections and access to all the best materials/sources.	

BOTTOM LINE

The adage "you get what you pay for" is why many couples prefer to hire a proven professional. They may cost more, but you can expect to receive a higher level of service, quality, and professionalism. Just make sure you feel a connection with the vendor and that their overall style aligns with yours.

NEWBIE PRO
New to their craft and/or the wedding industry

Why You Hire Them	What to Be Aware Of
• They may charge less for their services because they want to build their portfolio and reputation.	• Lack of experience combined with an eagerness to say yes can result in a failure to deliver as promised (i.e., biting off more than they can chew).
• They may be willing to do more for you or throw in extras at no additional cost.	• They may not have enough experience to know what could go wrong. This can mean no Plan B or Plan C or an inability to handle unforeseen situations on the fly.
• They may be willing to invest a lot of their personal time to get it right, and you benefit from their drive to succeed.	• Lack of business experience can potentially complicate interactions related to your contract, payments, etc.
• New talent can mean exciting and fresh new ideas for your wedding.	

BOTTOM LINE

There is a lot of great talent out there, and everyone has to start somewhere. It's a matter of your comfort level. It could be the best decision you've ever made! But if you are risk-averse, don't test out a newbie in your top priority areas.

DIY (DO-IT-YOURSELF)
You and whoever you can recruit for the job (friends, family)

Why You Hire Them

- You will potentially save a lot of money because you're not paying for the labor, knowledge, and services of a professional.

- You are a naturally gifted organizer and/or crafty person who is excited to be hands-on in the process and add your personal touch to the wedding.

- You are a professional in your field (e.g., graphic designer, event planner, pastry chef, etc.) and would like to apply your knowledge, skills, and resources to the task.

What to Be Aware Of

- You may potentially spend as much or more money as you would for a professional because you miscalculated how much it would cost or made costly mistakes.

- The amount of time needed to effectively research, source, and produce something—and do it right—is more than with professionals.

- You don't know the ins and outs of working a wedding and the logistics involved (delivery, setup/break down, liability, other insider knowledge, etc.). These details can make or break your DIY experience.

- Know what you can produce ahead of time (favors, invitations, etc.) versus what you can't (cake, food, flowers, etc.).

- You are not only the one getting married, you're also the vendor—which can be overwhelming on your wedding day.

BOTTOM LINE

DIY-ing can be an option if you're looking to save money and bring a personal touch to your wedding. Just make sure you've done your research and know exactly how much time, energy, and money it's going to take to produce what you want, at the quality you want. DIY disasters are usually a result of poor planning and a lack of knowledge about what's really involved in the process.

Sealing The Deal

You've met a vendor you love and feel like it's a match. Now it's time to seal the deal! Contracts are a standard part of doing business for any wedding professional. No money should ever be exchanged until you have one in place. If your vendor is a friend or family member, you may think you don't need one, but we recommend that you do put one in place. Put your agreement in writing and have both parties sign it, or at least put the terms in an email with both parties' acknowledgment. A contract sets a professional tone. The last thing you need is a ruined relationship if something goes wrong. A contract is there for both your protection and the vendor's. Every professional contract should include:

✓ Vendor name and contact details, including the point of contact

✓ Your name and contact details

✓ Date of service (day of week and date)—we recommend including the day of the week to be absolutely certain there is no mistake

✓ Description of the services or products being provided

✓ What products/services can be modified from the original contract and any deadlines to do so

✓ The cost of the services or products provided

✓ Deposit and payment schedule

✓ Additional fees that may be incurred, depending on the circumstances

✓ Amount due and payment terms (including how the vendor would like to be paid: cash, credit card, or personal check)

✓ Taxes and gratuity (this can add up, so make sure you know what the final amount will be)

✓ Details on logistics (expectations for delivery, time needed for set up, etc.)

✓ Cancellation, postponement, or return policies

✓ Force majeure (unforeseeable circumstances) policy

✓ When/if prices are guaranteed—if you are booking a wedding two years out and budgeting based on current pricing, you should confirm pricing is guaranteed

✓ If you are hosting an outdoor event, ensure there is an indoor (backup) space reserved for you and that it is on the contract (venue permitting)

✓ Any incentives or special promotions that were agreed upon

Provide as many details as possible in the contract. The more you have in writing, the better. Having specifics spelled out in the contract is incredibly useful when you're deep in the planning stages and can't quite remember what you agreed to five months earlier.

Another basic tip that we hope everyone knows is: *always* read the contract, *including the fine print*, before signing. If you don't understand a particular term or clause—ask. This is the time to clarify. It is important to understand your financial responsibility if your wedding cannot happen as planned due to an unforeseen situation, like a pandemic or a catastrophic event. If the year 2020 has taught us anything, it's that anything can happen. Plan for it. Then, after you've read everything and all your questions have been answered, both parties will sign the agreement to make it binding. Be sure to get a copy of the executed (i.e., signed) agreement for your reference.

Unexpected Costs

You may feel like you're constantly getting hit with unexpected costs while wedding planning. Most likely it has nothing to do with your contract. The number one reason for unexpected costs is that sometimes things happen that you didn't predict, which brings us back to . . .

You don't know what you don't know:
You can research and plan perfectly and still get hit with surprise expenses. This is the biggest reason we advised you in Chapter 4 to pad your final budget by at least 20%. There are things you can't anticipate or didn't know you needed when you made your initial budget. It's that moment when you realize:

• You absolutely need the venue's bridal room for an additional cost of $1,000 for four hours. With 10 people in your wedding party, it's the only practical solution for getting everyone's hair and makeup done in time by the stylists you've hired.

- The one photographer you hired won't be able to capture all the moments you want. There are many times throughout the day that you will want to see what is happening in different locations. For example, you don't want to miss the photos of both you and your partner getting ready in separate rooms, or your expressions from opposite ends of the aisle at the beginning of the ceremony. It's time to hire a second photographer.
- Your wedding attire needs additional alterations.
- The reception is going strong, so you ask the DJ to play for an extra hour, which means not only that you have to pay for their time, but for the additional time at the venue as well.
- The elaborate setup required for your ceremony and reception means your florist has to gain access into your venue earlier than anticipated, which extends your rental hours.
- The base pricing from your videographer doesn't cover all you want, so you decide to upgrade your package to include a longer film and custom music.
- You didn't plan enough for taxes or gratuity for each vendor, which can sometimes cost upwards of 25% of the total.
- You didn't give enough consideration to the transportation, and now you want to hire a bus to shuttle guests from the ceremony to the reception location.
- You decide to have a second guest list, so you need to order more invitations with a different RSVP date.

These are just a few of the many ways that weddings can upend your budget. Most times you can't plan for it, but you can prepare. The padding built into your budget should provide enough wiggle room to accommodate many of these expenses without going over budget. But don't go hog wild—the padding is there to address the unexpected, *not* for impulse shopping.

Summary

When it comes to assembling your vendors, the first decision is whether to use a wedding planner. A wedding planner is the general contractor for your event. They can oversee the entire process, and their job is to make sure your day goes seamlessly.

After the wedding planner, secure the rest of your vendors. Compile your vendor list. Start with your biggest priorities and work your way down.

Ways to find vendors:

- Hire a planner.
- Tap your network of family and friends for recommendations.
- Ask for preferred vendor lists from your venue.
- Find out who your venue manager's favorite vendors are.
- Get recommendations from other vendors.

Vetting your vendors means letting it all hang out. Share your budget and wedding vision portfolio. Have an honest conversation about what's possible and solicit their ideas. Determine whether the potential vendor is someone you'd like to work with and is excited to work on your wedding.

More tips for vetting your vendors:

- Check online reviews. Visit the vendor's website and social media. Look for examples of the wedding you envision.
- Verify whether the vendor is an established business.
- Research whether the vendor belongs to any professional or trade organizations.
- Find out whether the vendor specializes in weddings.
- Ask the vendor for their schedule—how many weddings do they typically do per weekend, month, or year?
- Get contact information for your point person.

Be aware of these red flags when vetting a vendor:
- Nonresponsiveness
- Lack of genuine interest
- Sloppy and slapdash behavior

Best advice for creating a productive vendor-client relationship:
- Be open-minded.
- Be honest.
- It's OK to ask.
- Be patient.

Important steps to take:
- Weigh the trade-offs between hiring a seasoned professional versus newbie professional versus DIY.
- Make your final decision on which vendors to hire.
- Read the contract carefully before signing and include as many details as possible about the services and products to be provided.
- Use the additional 20 to 35% padding in your budget to cover unexpected wedding costs.

CHAPTER

7

THE

Big Day

Last-minute issues always come up. No amount of planning can prevent them. Remember, this is a live event. Think of it like a play. No matter how much you rehearse, you never quite know how it's going to go on opening night.

Congratulations, you've made it! If you've followed our REAL DEAL Wedding Insider steps, then you've arrived at your wedding feeling prepared and in control. You're ready to share your commitment and vision with your friends and family. Wedding planning is never without its bumps, but you've minimized the biggest stressors using the Three Cs: having honest **communication** with your Wedding Committee, gaining real **comprehension** of your priorities, and making an accurate **calculation** of what your wedding will cost.

Now it's time to focus on your wedding day (or days, as many celebrations stretch into weekend-long events). With your wedding finally in sight, we hope you're feeling the love and anticipation of this milestone event. You've invested an enormous amount of time, money, thought, and emotion. The only thing left to do is *enjoy the day*. You want to minimize last-minute situations and stay present and focused on what really matters.

If you've ever hosted any kind of party, you know that you can carefully plan, clean, buy food and alcohol in advance, and still end up running around at the last minute. You can't fully relax. There's the food, the alcohol, the cleaning, the set up—the list goes on. This might be okay for a party, but it's *not okay* for your wedding. It's one day when you should absolutely be in the moment and let other people take care of the worrying.

Day-Of Management And Logistics

Weddings are multistaged events. Every detail is planned and timed in advance: ceremony, photos, cocktails, receiving line, dinner, entertainment, toasts, special dances, cake cutting, etc. It involves directing dozens (or hundreds) of guests. Given all of this, relaxing at your own wedding is a lot easier said than done. You're going to need the help of one or more point people. Their role is to ensure everything comes together smoothly, to troubleshoot problems, and to field questions so you don't have to. Leave the confused guests, missing signage, late arrivals, and lost bouquets to a person who can deal with it all quickly and efficiently!

WHAT NEEDS MANAGING

You need help. But before you think about who is going to help you, you need to figure out what needs managing. Every wedding is different, but in general there are eight areas to consider:

Timeline: Communicating the same timeline to all vendors the week of the event is crucial. This should include what time all vendors are arriving for setup, what length of time they're contracted for, and what time they're departing. Your venue or caterer should provide you with a timeline of food service (cocktail hour, first course, entrée, and dessert. You should know what time (roughly) food will be served and when it will be complete. This will ensure you know how long you have for dancing, formalities, etc. Your timeline should start well before the ceremony, maybe even days before if you need to schedule to-do's such as picking up rings or dropping off items at your venue with time to get to your rehearsal dinner. Your day-of vendors will be asking about timing to prepare their schedule for your day. For example, stylists need to know what time your photographer needs you "camera ready." The photographer will need to know how much time they have to get those must-have shots before the ceremony.

Sharing the contact information of vendors and wedding party members with the point person (wedding planner, venue contact, personal friend) is extremely important. What if the photographer gets a flat tire on their way to the ceremony? They may only have your email address or cell phone number. Do you want to worry about them contacting you while you're drinking a mimosa and rehearsing your vows? No, you want them to contact someone who can quickly communicate and resolve the issue without you needing to worry about it.

Vendors: If you've hired professional vendors, they'll know how to do their jobs, work with the venue, and coordinate with other vendors as necessary. You shouldn't have to worry about managing them. However, they'll likely have questions on the big day, especially if the unexpected happens (a sudden change in weather, a sickness, etc.). If you're incorporating DIY elements (centerpieces or decorative touches such as photos of you and your partner), they'll likely require coordination with certain vendors. Decisions will have to be made on the spot. Good vendors know this and are flexible. They always have a backup plan, but they need a point person on-site to answer questions and help assess situations as they arise.

Immediate family and wedding party: There's usually a flurry of activity that happens throughout the big day: "Here's my purse. Can you put it someplace safe?" "Can someone round up the groomsmen for photos?" "Can you check on Aunt Eleanor? She said she'd be here by now!" "I need extra bobby pins." "Can you get me something to eat?" All these requests add up to a lot of running around. But there's another kind of support that's equally as important as having people to run these errands—emotional support.

Weddings are highly charged events that can intensify emotions. You may want to have someone whose job it is to keep difficult people away from you, or at the very least, to run interference. Think about person-alities in advance. Is it possible an estranged relative might act out or someone in the wedding party might drink too much and cause an un-comfortable situation? Consider having a trusted person ready to deal with these issues so you don't have to.

Children and animals: W.C. Fields famously said, "Never work with children or animals." Turns out, that can be pretty good advice for weddings, too. If you thought a year ago that it would be adorable to have three-year-old ring bearers and flower girls, you will need someone to watch them before the ceremony. Are they where they're supposed to be? Are they on the verge of a meltdown? A growing trend is including fur babies in the festivities. If you want your dog in the wedding ceremony, that definitely requires assistance. Remember, you don't want to be picking up poop five minutes before walking down the aisle. Be sure you have handlers who can wrangle any kids or do doggie duty.

Set up and break down: Setting up can be a lot of work. Everything you're bringing to the venue (gift bags, favors, signs, guest book, framed pictures, etc.) has to be placed just so. After the wedding, you'll be expected to remove all belongings and DIY paraphernalia from the premises, most likely the same evening. This is not necessarily the responsibility of your vendors. At some traditional venues, where weddings are the key business, the venue manager may be willing to help you set up and pack up. You need to know beforehand what type of help you can expect and from whom. You'll need an on-site point person that knows where everything is going, oversees the set-up process, and makes certain everyone is on task (again, this point person is not you). You will also need a person or people who are willing to stick around at the end of the night to pack everything up (like all those wedding gifts!) and transport it somewhere safe, if need be.

Ceremony: Most ceremonies include a highly choreographed procession involving multiple groups of people, precisely timed music, and quite a bit of anticipation and nerves. Someone needs to be in charge so the procession runs smoothly. You want to be sure tasks like straightening the train of your dress and making sure flower girls have their headpieces on straight are not forgotten in the excitement. The clergy person or officiant knows how to do their part and will likely give you instructions for how the ceremony will run, but on the day of, they will be focused on their role not procession logistics. It sounds easy, but in those final moments before the ceremony, people are excited and moving around. That's when details are overlooked.

If your ceremony will take place at a traditional venue, your venue manager will often run the ceremony. The same holds true for a church, synagogue, or other place of worship. But in some cases, you're on your own. We recommend having a trusted point person to help with the ceremony. This should be someone who knows your family and is familiar with the ceremony details.

Transportation: In a weekend of many events, there may be numerous activities that require organized transportation. Often couples have their ceremony at one location and the reception at another. We recommend point people to manage the logistics on both ends of the trip. Having people on duty to answer questions, check to make sure all guests are accounted for, and direct traffic is invaluable. The last thing you want are frustrated, confused, or lost guests.

Your guests: Guess what? Even when you provide guests with all the information they need (including maps, event timeline, and contact information) on your wedding website or in their welcome bag, there will still be people who don't read it thoroughly (or at all) or get confused. You can't control everything, but the more complex your wedding—like multiple events at different locations—the more important it is to have someone on site to point guests in the right direction during transitional moments like moving from the ceremony to the reception.

The Who: Your Point People

Once you figure out what needs day-of support, it's time to think about who will provide it. How many and what type of point people you have will vary depending on your preference, venue, and financial situation. Here are some options:

Wedding planner: If you hire a full-service wedding planner or a professional day-of coordinator, you're getting support for all of the above categories and more. Many wedding planners offer day-of assistance as a separate package. The advantage of having a wedding planner is their experience. They anticipate problems and know how to avoid them. They know all the tips and tricks to keep things moving smoothly and on schedule. As a bonus, if they've worked your venue before, then they'll be familiar with the unique quirks of that venue.

A full-service wedding planner will have worked with you through-out the planning process, while a professional day-of coordinator usually gets involved four to eight weeks prior to the event. Both will help create the timeline for your event, coordinate with vendors, and provide direc-tion and support for every aspect of the big day. They will be the first ones on site to oversee set up and the last ones to leave, packing up your DIY items, gifts, and other belongings. They will check on grandma, bus-tle your dress, and make sure you don't walk down the aisle on an empty stomach. Their knowledge can help put you at ease. They can also pro-vide support during the rehearsal dinner or other activities, depending on the agreement you've made with them.

Venue manager at a traditional venue: One big advantage of getting married at a traditional venue is the support you'll receive on your wedding day. Because weddings are a huge percentage of a traditional venue's business, the venue managers are highly experienced. It's their job to ensure your event runs smoothly, with each part—ceremony, cocktail hour, and reception—occurring according to schedule. Also, it's likely they have established relationships with many of your vendors and know how to work with them. Ask the venue manager ahead of time what level of help you can expect on the big day.

Venue manager at a unique space: Most managers of museums, historic sites, libraries, and other unique wedding venues are in charge of the space, not your wedding. On the day of, their role is to protect the space, whether it's the artwork in the museum, the furniture in a historic mansion, or the animals in the zoo. They'll be on site to direct vendors to the right location and answer logistical questions, but they are not often involved in the wedding itself. However, as more unique spaces get into the wedding business, some have started to offer additional services. If your venue has such an option, find out exactly what they'll manage. If there isn't such an option, then the management of the event will fall to you and the caterer or the wedding planner, if you've hired one.

Catering manager at a unique space or alternative venue: In venues where there is not an additional experienced point person on site (such as a wedding planner or venue manager), your caterers often become the unofficial, de facto event manager. They are a natural point of contact, fielding questions, coordinating with other vendors, and overseeing the execution of the event timeline. It's important to ask what additional help they offer beyond the catering service.

Friends and family: These are usually your informal helpers rather than official point people, but they provide invaluable practical and emotional support on your wedding day. You could have anywhere from one helper to a mini army of helpers, depending on the level of support you're getting elsewhere and the number of DIY projects you've planned. Many couples have at least one person they can count on: the "doer" who is on board to run errands, make sure relatives get to where they're supposed to be, round up folks for a photo (they know who Uncle Paul is, while your photographer may not), and intervene in a family crisis. It could be a Confidant, bridesmaid, close family member, or friend. If you have someone like this in your circle, consider yourself lucky!

However, no matter how supportive your friends and family say they'll be on the day of your wedding, they want to have fun and enjoy themselves too. Be thoughtful about how much work you assign them. They are not your hired help. Even if they have the best of intentions, they can get distracted because *it's not their job to manage your wedding.* They may get sidetracked on their way to get the ring from the groom's room or could be in the bathroom instead of recording the bridesmaid's toast as promised.

If the job is really important, then hire (and pay) someone. It can be a responsible teenager to help with easier tasks (like corralling young kids or taking care of a dog) or a professional event helper for those tasks that require experience and focus. The more intricate and personalized your wedding is, the greater possibility that something can go wrong. Review your event timeline, make a list of what needs to get done from set up to break down, and then hire people who'll be there to work if you want to be certain the job gets done.

Tips For Staying Present

Your wedding day will be a whirlwind of activity and emotions. Taking the time to appreciate what's happening—as it's happening—is key for staying present in the moment. Faster than you can imagine, the day you've been planning and dreaming about for months (or years) will be over. You'll have videos and photographs to look back upon, but nothing replaces the actual experience. Here are our favorite tips to get the most out of your wedding day:

Make sure to eat and drink (hydrate with nonalcoholic drinks): Remembering to eat and drink may seem incredibly obvious, but when it's your wedding day, it can easily slip your mind, especially if you're busy or nervous.

Imagine, you're having your hair and makeup done starting at 11:00 a.m. and your first look is at 2:00 p.m. Your ceremony is at 4:30 p.m., then cocktail hour doesn't start until 5:00 p.m. Assuming you'll be talking, taking pictures, and touching up your makeup, you likely won't eat a lot during that time. You then go straight into announcements, the first dance, and other formalities. You may not start eating your first course until 6:30 or 7:00 p.m., assuming you're not out of your seat visiting tables at that time. You really want to give yourself energy (beyond adrenaline) to get you through the entire day without headache or fatigue.

Make sure you eat a healthy lunch if it's an evening wedding. Light snacks should be available to you throughout the day as you get ready. Also, you don't want to start drinking alcohol on an empty stomach, so remember to eat before you start the party! Another good rule of thumb is to alternate alcoholic drinks with water or another nonalcoholic beverage to make sure you're staying hydrated.

Schedule a private moment (or two) with your partner: Set aside time for you and your spouse to focus on each other and share a few moments away from the noise and attention of others. Of course, you can do this any time during your wedding, but it helps to schedule it into your timeline, so it's planned and purposeful. There are two popular options for this private time: the first look and a time following the ceremony.

Traditionally, it was considered bad luck for a couple to see each other before the ceremony. Nowadays, many couples are ignoring that superstition and scheduling a private moment for a "first look" before the ceremony. We are all for tradition, but there are reasons why a first look is really practical.

First looks are a great opportunity for your photographer to capture some of the sweetest, most fun images of the wedding. It's the moment you and your partner see each other in your wedding attire for the first time, so it's really special. After the photographs have been taken, the two of you can then spend a few quiet moments together before the ceremony. You can also opt to take many photos of the two of you and your wedding party before the wedding, so you can all enjoy the cocktail hour rather than pose for photos. You've spent so much time and energy planning this event—do you really want to miss any of it?

Another benefit: Your hair and makeup will be perfect, and you'll have time to freshen it up before the ceremony.

If you're worried that seeing your partner prior to the ceremony will take away from the excitement, we'd like to assure you it adds to your experience of the ceremony because you can be more present. It's pretty nerve-wracking walking down the aisle with all eyes on you. If you've already seen your partner, you'll be more settled and less distracted. You might not be as overwhelmed because you will have already had your private time with your partner to express your feelings, laugh or cry, and get some of the jitters out. Doing all that beforehand allows you to notice your guests as you walk down the aisle and take in the vows during the ceremony. We've convinced many couples to do a first look, and afterward they've said it was the best decision (and it didn't cost a thing).

If a first look still doesn't appeal to you, you may decide to spend a few quiet moments together immediately after the ceremony. Discuss with the venue whether there is a private room to share time together as a married couple before entering the festivities.

Schedule a sneak peek of your reception: Schedule a time to look at the reception room after it's set up and before your guests enter. Take a few minutes to see your room design in all its glory. Make sure your photographer is there as well to capture the décor while it's pristine.

Thank your guests: Whether you visit each table, stand in a receiving line, or make an announcement during the reception, you should carve out time to acknowledge your guests. Express gratitude that they've taken time out of their lives to celebrate your union. Gratitude is part of staying present on your wedding day.

Give a "time out" to technology: There's no getting away from technology and social media, and for the most part, it's a fun way to document your wedding and engage with guests (and those who couldn't attend). However, some things should remain sacred or at least have boundaries put around them. When you're walking down the aisle and exchanging vows, you want your guests to be in the moment with you, instead of focusing on their personal devices. Before the ceremony begins, have the officiant ask your guests to shut off cell phones and other devices to keep the clicks, flashes, and other distractions to a minimum. This is often referred to as an "unplugged ceremony." It also helps the professional photographer and videographer do their jobs without competing with the guests trying to capture the moment with their phones. In your printed program, include a request to silence all cell phones during the ceremony as well. If you want your ceremony live-streamed in real time, arrange to have someone do that for you beforehand.

Don't rush your honeymoon: There's no rule that says you have to go on your honeymoon the day after your wedding. Avoid the additional stress of thinking about airports and packing as you walk down the aisle by leaving for your honeymoon a few days (or even weeks or months) later. This allows you more relaxed time with family and friends immediately following your wedding.

Summary

Wedding day management should be taken care of by people other than you and your partner so you can stay present and fully appreciate the day. What needs managing?

1. **Timeline:** It's important to create a timeline for the entire day so that all wedding participants and vendors know where they need to be and when.

2. **Vendors:** Vendors need an on-site point person to answer questions and help address unexpected issues as they occur.

3. **Immediate family and wedding party:** These folks need a trusted person to take care of personal requests and help keep unwanted drama away from you.

4. **Children and animals:** Make sure to have someone on hand who can keep both kids and furry friends in check during the ceremony.

5. **Set up and break down:** You'll need someone to set up your DIY projects prior and help collect them at the end of your event.

6. **Ceremony:** You need someone in charge of the ceremony procession to ensure small details don't get overlooked.

7. **Transportation:** You'll want point people on both ends of the journey to manage the flow of guests.

8. **Guests:** You'll want point people to direct your guests during key moments of the event.

Potential Point People

1. Wedding planner or
   day-of wedding coordinator
2. Venue manager
3. Catering manager
4. Family and friends
5. Hire responsible friend
   or other individual(s)

   The more nontraditional your venue and
   unique the activities planned, the more you'll need
   help to ensure a seamless execution of your event.

Tips for staying present during your wedding:

1. Eat and hydrate well before the festivities begin.

2. Schedule a private moment (or two) with your partner.
   We love either a "first look" before or scheduled private
   moments immediately following the ceremony.

3. Schedule a sneak peek of the venue prior to
   guests arriving.

4. Thank your guests.

5. Limit technology.

6. Don't rush your honeymoon.

To learn more about Real Deal Wedding Insiders® visit:

www.realdealweddinginsiders.com

@WeddingInsiders
@RealDealWeddingInsiders
@RealDealWeddingInsiders

ACKNOWLEDGMENTS

We are so grateful to those who lent their talents, creativity and insight to help bring our book to fruition. Sharon Dratch Edwards, Lauren Phipps, Jyotirmayee Patra, Stacey Endress, Shana Cinquegrana, Turku Hasturk, Terry Heyman, Keira Campbell, Kim Ledgerwood, Jill Gallagher, Lisa Tynan and Kathleen Quinton, at every point in the process your contributions were invaluable.

To our couples—it is an honor and pleasure guide you through your planning journey and see your joy on your wedding day. We learn from each and every one of you.

We are proud to be a part of the larger wedding and event community. A special thanks to the Boston Wedding Group and its members (an organization that is close to our hearts), NACE Boston, and ILEA Boston. These organizations allow us to grow, network, learn and be a part of the deep fabric the Boston event world.

From Edna

To my family: my parents, Morris and Gladys, and sisters Annette and Sharon, who have encouraged me through every venture and dream as far back as I can remember. It's easy to love the wedding world when you have parents whose marriage is an inspiration! For my husband Jim … you have my heart! Thank you for your support not only in my ventures, but helping onsite at weddings. Love you!

From Jeri

I'm so lucky to have people in life that support, love and celebrate my endeavors. Thanks to my extended family, aka The Significant Crew, my confidante Alex, my son, Jason, and my husband, Jim. ("It Had To Be You!")

Made in United States
Troutdale, OR
01/15/2024

16948197R00082